·················

DESIGNING
WITH
HOUSEPLANTS

·················

Alan Toogood

EDITED BY CAROLE HUPPING

GALLERY BOOKS

A QUINTET BOOK

Published by Gallery Books
An imprint of W. H. Smith Publishers, Inc.,
112 Madison Avenue
New York, New York 10016

ISBN 0-8317-46009

This book was designed and produced by
Quintet Publishing Limited
6 Blundell Street
London N7 9BH

Creative Director: Peter Bridgewater
Art Director: Ian Hunt
Designers: Stuart Walden, Louise Morley
Project Editors: David Game and Sally Harper
Editor: Carole Hupping
Picture Researcher: Ruth Sonntag
Illustrations on pages 24, 25, 38, 39, 48, 49, 58, 59
Danny McBride
Artwork: Jenny Millington

Typeset in Great Britain by
Central Southern Typesetters, Eastbourne
Manufactured in Hong Kong by
Regent Publishing Services Limited
Printed in Hong Kong by
Leefung-Asco Printers Limited

CONTENTS

INTRODUCTION

Houseplants are a wonderful way to help make indoor spaces warm and attractive. They literally bring life to any room they're placed in and make us all feel a bit closer to nature. Because they are relatively inexpensive and come in so many different shapes, sizes and even colours, they can 'decorate' a room easily and quickly, adding dramatic focal points and background interest. They can bring a splash of colour to a dull spot, draw the eye away from a disappointing view out the window, hide a defect on the wall, create a mood.

Because houseplants are so inviting they naturally encourage impulse-buying. A stately palm catches your eye at an outdoor market and you imagine it gracing that empty spot next to your living room sofa. That zebra plant, in full golden bloom, would look wonderful in the dark corner of your hallway. The maidenhair fern, so big and healthy, is just the thing for a hanging pot at the bright dining room window.

But such impulse-buying can lead to disasters. (Indeed it would, if you chose a light-demanding zebra plant for a shady spot or a delicate fern for a sunny one.) It can mean choosing plants that you would like to have for particular places without considering whether those places would be the best homes for the plants, whether they would provide suitable conditions for keeping them happy and healthy. If the room temperature is too warm or too cool, the air too dry or the spot too dark, that lovely plant you bring home may become weak and die or go on living but grow dull and look miserable.

Your plants would be much better off and you'd be happier in the long run if you took a bit of time and thought to buy houseplants that matched the growing conditions provided by your rooms. Luckily, this is not really very difficult to do at all. There are more than a hundred plants for you to choose from and probably dozens that are suitable for every room in your house.

Design-consciousness is hardly the sole reserve of interior designers today. Books, magazines, television and home shows have made us all aware of how beautiful interior spaces can really be. Few people are any longer content to have a few potted plants dotted around the window sill. Plants can play an integral role in the design of a room, often matching the colour scheme and enhancing the decor. Large, dramatic specimen plants create striking local points; plants can be hung from the ceiling or walls; and large groups of foliage and flowering plants create attractive living room features. Suitable methods of displaying plants are fully described in this book. You will also discover more unusual ways to create room features. These include how to grow plants in illuminated glass cases or terrariums and how to train climbing plants up moss poles and wall trellises.

The success of such displays depend on the vital aspects of plant care: watering, feeding and potting, and in the chapters following you will find information on just what care each of the plants included in the book need and how to provide it. Many people like to propagate some of their own plants, and there is information on how to do this, covering every method practical at home, from growing from seed, to growing from cuttings and to air-layering. Houseplants, though less threatened than outdoor plants, are not completely immune to pests and diseases, and the book ends with a chapter on the detection, control and the elimination of the most common of these.

With more than 170 houseplants to choose from in these pages, you will find one for every situation in your home — even for a few seemingly impossible places!

LEFT The stark lines of this area are echoed in the dragon plant, and suitably softened with a group of smaller plants clustered at its base.

1

....

*S*UCCESSFUL *DISPLAYS IN LIVING ROOMS*

....

LEFT False aralia is a fine specimen plant. It grows slowly, however, so if you want a large one, like the one here, buy a good-sized plant to start with. A sunny window is an ideal spot.

The living room is the most 'public' room in the house, it is where you entertain, where friends gather and enjoy your home and company. So you want it to look especially good, to reflect your personality and taste.

Houseplants can work wonders in a living room, creating just the environment you want. There are many places you could put them. It is probably the largest space in your house. There may be both high and low tables on which plants would look wonder-ful. Perhaps there are bookshelves with room to spare and even empty corners on the floor that could do with a few tall plants. If those corners are darker than they should be for plants, you can illuminate the space with one or more small spotlights hidden discreetly among the plants or behind furniture. Or you could install track lighting on the ceiling to shine down on to the plants. Such lighting can look very dramatic as it reflects off the shapes and colours of plant leaves.

ABOVE Suitable specimen plants for the living room include the parasol plant (left), the dwarf orange (centre) and dragon lily (right). The last mentioned will grow into a tall plant, suitable for use as a floor specimen.

Aesthetically the living room may be just right for houseplants, but practically speaking, the room can be one of the most difficult places to grow houseplants. This is because the high temperatures usually maintained in a living room make the air very dry, causing the leaves to turn brown at the edges or even to shrivel up completely.

Constant heat can also cause leaves and flower-buds to fall off. Another problem faced by living room-sited plants is the fact that daytime temperatures in the living room range from 18 to 24°C (65 to 75°F) and at night they may fall to between 13 and 15.5°C (55 and 60°F). Such temperatures are fine for many plants, provided they are allowed enough humidity or moist air around them.

Never water or mist plants last thing at night, however. Plants which will happily withstand cold, dry conditions will be killed by a combination of cold and damp. There are various ways of displaying plants in an attractive way in living rooms, some of which generate their own supply of humidity to encourage growth, making care both simple and foolproof.

One way is to group plants together, either by clustering separate pots together on a table or the floor, or by potting several plants together in one large container (see the section Groups in Large Planters which comes a bit later). The moisture in the soil in the pots and the water vapour given off by the leaves of the plants themselves during transpiration will keep the air right around the plants more humid than that in the rest of the room. You can also increase humidity by sitting plant pots on plates or shallow dishes that contain marbles or gravel. Keep the marbles or gravel wet at all times.

In winter, when the heating is on, living room air can get very dry. To minimize this problem, you may wish to place shallow bowls or pots filled with water in inconspicuous places around the room and especially near radiators. The water, as it evaporates in the warmth of the air, will increase the overall humidity of the space, benefiting the plants as well as the people and furniture there too. All will be better off if the air isn't excessively dry.

BELOW The understated look of this room provides a striking environment for plants. Since there is little to compete with them, they stand out, particularly the tall dragon tree next to the window.

BELOW LEFT Young plants of various kinds are useful as table specimens. The plant on the left is a dieffenbachia or dumb cane, with heavily mottled foliage, and the one on the right the ever-popular weeping fig.

LEFT Large specimen plants are often favoured for living rooms as they can act as focal points, drawing the eye to some particular part. Many of the palms are ideal for this purpose, such as the thatch palm. Climbing plants such as cissus (right), trained to a cane, also make excellent large specimens.

FAR LEFT Grouping plants not only often looks more striking than setting plants about individually, it also can mean a healthier plant environment. This is because the humidity in the air around a cluster of plants is greater than that around a single plant.

SPECIMEN PLANTS

Large specimen plants are often favoured for living rooms since they act as focal points, drawing the eye towards a particular spot. Well-grown houseplants are available at garden centres and florists. Don't bother trying to grow your own large plants from small ones. With few exceptions you won't have much luck. Large plants are usually specific large-plant varieties that grow big only in very warm and humid conditions such as you find in tropical parts of the world and in commercial greenhouses.

One houseplant you may have luck growing into a large specimen is the avocado plant, which you can grow from an avocado seed (pit or stone of the avocado pear). Start by suspending the large seed in a glass of water. Make sure the root end is just barely touching the edge of the water at all times.

With luck roots will grow from the seed and when they appear well established you can pot the seed with the roots down in some potting compound or soil and wait for green growth to emerge. Repot as the plant grows and keep in full sun if you want a healthy, tall and bushy plant.

Another tall houseplant that you can 'grow' is a plant tree, which is actually a tree cutting that is propped in a pot from which plants like air plants and bromeliads grow. (See the section Plant Trees in chapter 2.)

Because specimen plants are show-off plants you will most likely want to pot them in large ornamental pots or place the conventional pots in which they are growing in larger decorative containers. There are many different kinds of holders available, in china, pottery and plastic. Antique copper or brass containers of various kinds are a favourite, and you should be able to match them to the decor of your *room. The diameter of the pot holder should be greater than that of the pot and the space between the two should be filled with peat or some other moisture-retaining medium. This must be kept permanently moist so that even in dry conditions it will provide essential humidity around the plant.*

Some specimen plants may have to be supported so that they grow tall and straight and don't fall or bend over. All sorts of stakes – wood, cane, plastic and wire – can be bought at garden centres. Obviously you will want to buy one that will be as inconspicuous as possible for your plant. Be sure to push the stake right down to the bottom of the pot (avoiding injuring roots) to give it a good, sturdy base. Gently tie the stem or stems of your plant to the stake at several places with lengths of soft string.

You can purchase a green-coloured string at a garden centre just for this purpose. Avoid tying with wire or nylon thread; they can cut into delicate plant stems.

You can make some climbing houseplants 'stand up tall' by supporting them on a pole wrapped with moss. (See the section Moss Poles for Climbers later in this in chapter.)

Turn tall plants regularly so that one side is not always facing toward the main light source in the room. This will ensure that they grow tall and straight.

Plants which are to be used as specimen plants should be bold and distinctive, and the following are highly recommended.

RIGHT This wonderful pot in the shape of a snarling leopard's head is as much, if not more, of an eye-catcher as the stately date palm planted in it.

RIGHT This enormous Boston fern in its impressive stone urn makes a very bold statement and becomes the focal point of the room. A large side window provides the gentle light that it prefers.

1 Anthurium crystallinum ('strap flower'). This has large, velvety, deep-green leaves with silvery white hairs. It likes plenty of humidity and light.

2 Beaucarnea recurvata ('pony tail'). This unusual plant, with a swollen stem which slowly elongates, is topped with a rosette of thin, arching deep-green, grassy leaves. It needs bright light and a little sunshine.

Cissus antarctica ('kangaroo vine'). This favourite plant has large glossy leaves and grows to 10ft. Rhoicissus rhomboidea ('grapy ivy') – often called C.rhombifolia – and R.r. 'Ellen Danica' have shiny leaves growing in triplets; all make tolerant houseplants (page 11).

3 Citrus microcarpa ('dwarf orange' or calamondin). This produces small, bitter oranges and likes very bright light, including sunshine.

Cordyline terminalis ('cabbage palm', 'good-luck plant'). Long, broad leaves – bronze-red or red and green – gives this plant a palm-like appearance. It needs good light (page 66).

4 Dizygotheca elegantissima ('false aralia'). This shrubby plant with long, narrow, deep-copper leaves is a slow grower. So buy a large specimen. It likes plenty of humidity and bright light.

Dracaena ('dragon lily'). Palm-like shrubs of this plant come with green-and-white striped leaves in

D. deremensis 'Bausei' and **D. d.** 'Warneckii', and yellow-and-green striped leaves in the **D. fragrans** varieties. They like bright light.

Ficus. Among the most popular houseplants for use as specimens, these are the rubber and fig plants, which often reach as high as the ceiling very quickly! The most famous rubber plant is **5 F. elastica,** which has large, thick, dark-green, shiny leaves. Very popular is the 'weeping fig', **F. benjamina,** which has much smaller leaves and tends to arch as it grows. The 'fiddleback fig' or fiddle-leaf fig, **F. lyrata,** is dramatic, to say the least, with its huge spoon-shaped leaves. They like light or slight shade.

Heptapleurum arboricola 'Variegata' ('parasol plant'). A comparatively new houseplant with hand-shaped, yellow-splashed leaves; quickly grows into a large specimen. It needs bright light and good humidity

6 Howea forsteriana ('thatch palm'). This is a popular palm, though a slow-grower. Buy a largish specimen. It has somewhat pendulous, small leaves and will grow in either a well lit or a shady spot.

7 Pandanus veitchii ('screw pine'). This distinctive plant has sword-like leaves with stripes of dark green and white. It needs bright light and plenty of humidity.

Hanging Containers

Suspending plants in hanging pots is a very effective way of creating more space for plants indoors. Hanging plants can be positioned to complement houseplants on tables, shelves and window sills, or they can be the only plants in a room. They can be the solution to a problem window that provides the perfect light for plants but that has no window sill nor space nearby on the floor for plants. Hanging plants work very well suspended from the ceiling above or on walls next to french doors. (Just position them so that the doors can swing open freely.) They can be terribly dramatic when hung under skylights. (Because overhead light through skylights can be quite strong, choose plants that thrive in full sun.)

The most suitable indoor hanging baskets are the modern plastic ones which have built-in drop trays. Macramé holders, which are usually designed to hold several ceramic or plastic pots, one above the other, can look very pleasing. You can also get nylon thread for practically invisible support. The nylon, though thin, is extremely strong, and because you can hardly see the thread once it's in place, the pots suspended from it appear to be floating in air. Unlike jute and other natural fibres, nylon has the advantage that it is guaranteed to never rot, unravel or tear.

ABOVE A co-ordinated colour scheme in which the plants blend beautifully with the decor. This room features hanging baskets which contain asparagus ferns.

Because hanging pots, even the light plastic ones, can get very heavy when they are filled with moist potting soil or compost, be sure to mount them with properly sized brackets or hooks and a heavy enough weight of thread, wire or cord. Take care with the types of fixtures you use. Different wall surfaces will require different types of fasteners, as will ceilings. If you have used natural fibre cords for hanging your pots check them every now and then to be sure that there are no signs of wear or rot. Replace the cords if you're suspicious; a little prevention is better than having a cord break and its pot come crashing to the floor.

It is sometimes difficult to water the plants in hanging containers, but a watering-can with a long spout should overcome the difficulty. Since plants growing in indoor baskets are not naturally supplied with humidity, you should mist-spray the leaves daily. When using a hanging pot holder, ensure that the holder is wider than the pot and fill the space between the two with peat or another moisture-retaining medium, which must be kept moist.

Plants which have a habit of trailing or arching during growth are most suitable for hanging containers, especially since some of them have a colourful underside on their leaves, which is not visible if the plants are displayed at the lower level.

RIGHT A glass lantern, looking like a terrarium but with the sides open, is a handsome hanging container. It is filled with plants that will trail down as they grow: a variegated ivy, polka dot plant and strawberry geranium, or mother of thousands.

ABOVE To create a natural-looking hanging plant, choose a container made from a natural material and size it so that the plant is large enough to cover much of the container. Here, columnea has been planted in a plastic-lined wicker basket.

ABOVE A birdcage makes an interesting container for a small-leaved, heavy trailing plant such as the variegated ivy here.

Asparagus ('asparagus ferns'). These foliage plants are not true ferns, but they have a very fern-like or feathery appearance. The 'foxtail asparagus', **A. densiflorus** 'Myers', has vivid, green, arching plumes of foliage; **1 A. densiflorus** 'Sprengeri' has a habit of trailing and has bright, green, prickly-looking leaves. Both will grow in a moderately shady spot and both prefer a reasonable amount of humidity.

Callisia elegans. This trailer has green-and-white striped sleaves with purple undersides. It needs bright light and plenty of humidity (page 68).

2 Mikania ternata ('plush vine'). This is one of the latest trailing houseplants. It has hairy leaves with a purple underside. It prefers gentle shade and plenty of humidity.

3 Nephrolepsis exaltata ('sword fern'). Its arching, bright green fronds make this one of the best ferns for a hanging container. It needs plenty of humidity and soft shade.

Oplismenus hirtellus 'Variegatus'. The grass-like foliage of this trailing plant is striped with white, pink and green. It should be replaced regularly with younger plants, which are easily raised from cuttings. It needs plenty of light (page 69).

Peperomia scandens 'Variegata' ('pepper elder'). A trailing plant is variegated with yellow and green. It must be watered sparingly, as too much moisture will rot the roots. It needs either bright light or moderate shade (page 69).

4 Plectranthus oertendahlii ('candle plant'). This is a magnificent, trailing foliage plant; the leaves are dark green with white veins and the undersides are purple. It grows best in soft shade.

Scindapsus aureus ('devil's ivy'). One of the most popular trailing plants, it can also be used as a climber. Its leaves are splashed with either yellow or white. It will grow the best leaf-colour if you allow it plenty of light (page 69).

Setcreasea purpurea ('purple heart'). The vivid, purple leaves on this trailing plant are best displayed when the plant is in a hanging container. It needs plenty of bright light and should be renewed regularly from cuttings, which can be easily rooted in the growing season (page 67).

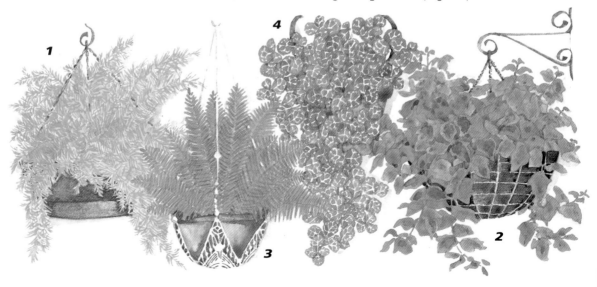

Stenotaphrum secundatum 'Veriegatum' ('buffalo grass'). This is a trailing plant with grass-like leaves which are striped with cream and green. The stems root into the soil, which makes propagation relatively simple, since all you have to do is detach the rooted stems and put them in the pot. It needs bright light and grows best in a shallow pot.

Syngonium podophyllum ('goose foot', 'arrowhead vine'). Can be grown as a trailer or a climber. Its arrow-shaped foliage is variegated in white and green or sometimes yellow and green. It needs soft shade and plenty of humidity (page 71).

Tradescantia ('wandering Jew'). This is a very popular trailing plant, which usually has variegated foliage. One of the most distinctive species is **T. fluminensis** 'Quicksilver', which has leaves with green and silver-white stripes. To produce the best colour it needs plenty of light.

Zebrina pendula ('wandering Jew'). This is similar in appearance to **Tradescantia.** Its leaves are banded with silver and green and the undersides are vivid purple. It needs plenty of light to allow it to produce the best colour.

TERRARIUMS AND OTHER GLASS GARDENS

Grouping small houseplants together under glass can make a lovely accent for a quiet place in your home. Like a piece of sculpture, but in this case a living piece of sculpture, a terrarium or other glass garden needs no accompaniments and is best set all by itself, on a simple table or shelf.

You could place it in a north-facing window or one that is shaded with an awning or transparent curtain, but avoid placing the terrarium in direct sunlight. The terrarium's glass both magnifies the rays of the sun shining on it and traps air warmed up by the sun inside. A terrarium softly lit from behind with a built-in light can be very effective, as can a soft spotlight from above shining on it.

Terrariums, especially the lovely handmade Victorian-looking ones (which were called Wardian cases in their time), can be expensive but they can be repotted over and over again, giving many years of pleasure. If you want something costing less, consider making your own from a fishtank, goldfish bowl, clear confectionery jar or large, old-fashioned

TOP This elegant terrarium is large enough to contain many plants.

ABOVE A tasteful homemade terrarium containing a young philodendron and dwarf sansevieria.

ABOVE A large jar is transformed into a piece of living sculpture. A delicate touch, patience and small, long-handled tools are necessary to pot the plants through such a narrow opening.

RIGHT This antique wrought-iron Wardian case protects delicate ferns from draughts and dry air and maintains the steady, humid environment which they prefer.

pickling jar. They can be totally enclosed or open at the top. Choose something made from clear or lightly tinted glass (preferably green); anything darker will keep out too much light.

Terrariums and other glass gardens involve a bit more work at the start than other plant groupings because of the need to arrange the planting medium, choose suitable plants that work well together and don't grow too quickly, determine how often, if at all, they need to be watered and how often to be fertilized. But once they are established they are very independent and need little attention.

One way to display plants together, especially the more delicate kinds which like plenty of warmth and high humidity, is in a glass case, or terrarium. There are many different kinds available, including very attractive ones shaped like small greenhouses. However, most terrariums are so small that only a few plants can be grown in them. They are also expensive.

As an alternative, you could buy a frameless glass fishtank, of the type available from tropical-fish dealers. These fishtanks come in a wide range of sizes and can be supplied with covers which have built-in fluorescent lighting. They make very effective terrariums, since the lighting helps plants to grow better and, at the same time, shows them to their best advantage. The display will also highlight a dark corner of a room.

A planted fishtank does not need any additional heat, so long as it is kept in a warm environment. The plants can be arranged so that the display resembles the floor of a tropical rain forest, which, after all, is the natural habitat of the most popular species.

To prepare the fishtank, give it a good wash and then make sure that it is dry inside. Once the tank is completely dry, pour a 2.5cm (1in) layer of shingle on the bottom to help drain off any surplus water. Over the shingle place a 7.5–10cm (3–4in) layer of peat-based potting medium (without soil).

The collection of plants should be planted in this 'soil'. Arrange the tallest ones at the back, with perhaps the next highest at the sides; then arrange the medium-height plants in the centre and the lowest at the front. This arrangement will ensure that all the plants are easily seen. To set the display

LEFT Jars of almost all shapes and sizes can be transformed into terrariums. Here you see a storage jar, a confectionery jar, a cider jug and a wine glass filled with living plants.

off nicely, place a few pieces of bark or branch among the plants, or even some deep-brown or blackish mangrove root, which is sold by tropical-fish dealers.

A planted fishtank needs very little attention, but you must remember to keep the 'soil' moist. Do not overwater. The surplus water cannot drain away and if it builds up in the bottom of the tank it will saturate the 'soil' and make it difficult for the plants to flourish. The 'soil' usually dries out very slowly; so frequent watering is not necessary. The moist compost should keep the atmosphere humid, but if you want to provide even more humidity, spray the plants lightly with water. Dead and dying leaves or flowers encourage diseases, such as grey mould or botrytis, and should be removed regularly.

Suitable plants for a fishtank include the 'earth stars', or *Cryptanthus,* which forms rosettes of colourful foliage, rather like a starfish. The best species are *C. zonatus* and *C. bivattatus*. Episcia hybrids, or flame violets, relish the warm, humid conditions of a tank. They have a low creeping habit, attractively marked leaves and colourful, tubular flowers.

Fittonia verschaffeltii, or 'mosaic plant', is a low, carpeting foliage plant with red-veined leaves.

There are also varieties with silver veins, such as *F.v.* 'Argyroneura' and *F.v.* 'Argyroneura Nana'.

The Saintpaulias, or African violets, are ideal for tanks, since they need very warm, humid conditions. These rosette-forming plants, which flower over a very long period each year, are highly popular and can be found in every garden centre or florist. They come in all shades of blue, purple, red, pink and white. Some varieties have single flowers; others are doubled. The new, miniature Saintpaulias are possibly better for tanks, since they take up less space than the more conventional kinds. Perhaps the best-known variety is 'Pip Squeek', which has pink blooms. You will have to buy miniatures from an African violet specialist.

Selaginella is a mossy or ferny foliage plant which forms low mounds of growth. The best-known and most easily available species is *S. kraussiana,* a creeping plant with attractive green foliage. Also worth looking out for is the yellow-green variety, *S.k.* 'Aurea'.

Another low-growing creeping foliage plant suitable for tanks is *Sonerila margaritacea,* whose deep green leaves are attractively splashed with white and have purple undersides. The leaves are carried on conspicuous red stems.

GROUPS IN LARGE PLANTERS

Groups of flowering and foliage plants placed in large planters can be very stunning and much more dramatic than a cluster of little potted plants sitting about individually. A large planter can become the focal point of the room if it is, for example, placed on a low central table in front of the sofa or a large low window, or in the fireplace when it's not in use.

The container you choose can make all the difference. Because it's most likely going to be a large and showy grouping, you might want to consider something a bit out of the ordinary. How about an old-fashioned copper water boiler or an enormous soup tureen? For Easter you may want to look for a giant handmade wicker basket. At Christmastime an old black kettle done up with red and green ribbons could be very nice. (Any of these — and most other containers you might choose — will have to be lined so that they are waterproof.)

Potting several plants together gives you a wonderful opportunity to match the colour scheme of your room by adding one flowering plant to the group or perhaps using one plant with strongly variegated or coloured leaves. You could also, of course, bring into the grouping some dried or silk flowers, a piece of sculpture or some found objects like driftwood or pine cones.

You can simply remove all the plants from their pots and plant them together in your larger container. But you might find it more satisfactory to keep each in its own pot surrounded by a moisture-retaining material made for the purpose. This way you can lift out any plant that you wish at any time and replace it, without disturbing the roots of neighbouring plants. Keep this in mind especially if you're putting a flowering plant into the group. Often a flowering plant, especially if forced into flower in a greenhouse, will lose its blooms after a few weeks and need to be replaced.

When you are thinking about what type of arrangement to make with your plants keep in mind the relative heights, shapes, colours and textures of them and work up an arrangement using many of the same considerations you do when arranging flowers in a basket or wide vase. You can arrange your groups so that they match the colour scheme of the room, or have a collection that complements the season.

ABOVE This wickerwork planter suits the room setting but must have an internal waterproof liner, such as a plastic bowl. A good selection of plants has been arranged around a Swiss cheese plant and a red-leaved cabbage palm.

RIGHT Springtime is the theme of these two lovely arrangements of flowers and foliage plants. Both planters are too small to have plants potted separately so they will have to be repotted when the blooms fade.

A planter may be square, rectangular, circular or even hexagonal. Most are plastic, although some are made of wood, in which case they must have a waterproof plastic liner inside. Planters for indoor use must not, of course, have drainage holes in the base, since water would run out and ruin the floor.

The planter should be filled with peat or another absorbent substance used by horticulturalists, which must be kept permanently moist so that a humid atmosphere will be maintained around the plants. Potted plants are plunged to the pot rims in the peat so the pots are completely hidden.

It is quite simple to arrange plants in a planter. If the group is to be viewed from all sides, arrange tall plants in the centre and graduate the plants, making them progressively smaller towards the edges. You could place trailing plants just inside the edges to cascade over the sides. If the planter is positioned against a wall, where it will be viewed from only one side, you could create a triangular effect by placing a tall plant in the centre and flanking it with progressively shorter plants. Alter-natively, you could arrange tall plants at one end of the planter and graduate to the opposite end with shorter plants. For extra effect, set trailers at the front and at each end.

With a group positioned against a wall, you must ensure that the background complements the plants. A heavily patterned wallpaper is defin-itely out, since the plants would merge into the background; a plain white or lightly coloured wall is ideal. A large mirror (or mirror tiles) makes an excellent background because it gives the illusion of depth and multiplies the plants; it also lights up the group. As for lighting, why not install spotlights to highlight the plants at night? Do not, however, use coloured lights, which make plants look unnatural.

The possible combinations of plants are almost limitless, but here are a few suggestions to start you off.

If you want a highly colourful winter arrange-ment for the living room, you can choose from an abundance of plants at Christmas time. You might

BELOW Small plants can mask the uninteresting base of an otherwise attractive specimen plant. Here a peacock plant, pilea and weeping fig are planted in a copper pot, which sits in front of the plain container holding a dwarf orange, giving the illusion that they are all planted together.

consider the poinsettia or *Euphorbia pulcherrima*, with its scarlet, leaf-like bracts. You could choose some foliage plants to contrast or blend with it, such as the false aralia. *Dizygotheca elegantissima* is a very attractive plant, with its deep-copper leaves, and it could be combined with the brown-banded *Vriesia splendens* ('flaming sword'), which has a scarlet, yellow-flowered head. The edge of the planter could be finished off with a trailing fig, *Ficus pumila* or *F.p. minima*, which has small, green leaves for good indoor ground cover.

If you want colour throughout the summer, combine a group of the *Hibiscus rosa-sinensis* species, which has large flowers in various shades of red, yellow or orange, with *Impatiens* 'New Guinea' hybrids, or 'busy lizzie', which sports a colourful foliage and bright flowers. Suitable foliage plants for this group include Codiaeums, or crotons, with their multi-coloured leaves; the peacock plant, *Calathea lancifolia*, in various shades of green; the prayer plant, *Maranta leuconeura* 'Kerchoveana', with red-brown blotches, and the ribbon fern, *Pteris cretica*, with feathery green foliage.

The 'shrimp plant', *Beloperone guttata*, produces pink, shrimp-like blooms for most of the year and is worth including in another group. Suitable foliage plants to complement it are the multicoloured *Begonia rex* and the iron-cross begonia, *B. masoniana*, each leaf of which has a bronze-purple cross in the centre. You could add the bronze-red cabbage palm, *Cordyline terminalis*, the variegated 'devil's ivy' (*Scindapsus aureus*) and the ever-popular Swiss cheese plant, *Monstera deliciosa*, with its perforated leaves.

MOSS POLES FOR CLIMBERS

You can buy a moss mole from shops, but it is easy to make your own. Insert a 6ft-long broom handle into a large clay pot filled with soil-based potting medium. Then place a cylinder of small-mesh wire netting over the handle, making sure that it is well below soil level, and pack the cylinder with live sphagnum moss. Insert a small pot into the top of the cylinder so that its rim is level with or below the netting. Water is regularly poured into this pot so that it trickles down through the moss, keeping it

ABOVE Because this fireplace has an attractive brass railing around it, no decorative planter is necessary. Poinsettia plants sit in their own pots with other foliage plants to create a Christmassy atmosphere.

RIGHT A simple but striking green and white theme is achieved in this fireplace grouping of delicate ferns on either side of a snake plant.

moist. Once this is done you can plant a suitable climber at the base of the moss pole.

Plants such as the monstera, philodendrons and scindapsus produce roots from their stems. These can be guided into the moss so that the plants support themselves. Another suitable plant is the Swiss cheese plant, Monstera deliciosa, with its perfor-

ated and deeply cut leaves. Many exotic-looking philodendrons are also suitable. Available species are P. angustisectum, P. bipennifolium, P. erubescens, P. hastatum, the ever-popular 'sweetheart vine' or 'heart-leaf philodendron' P. scandens, and P. 'Tuxla'. The 'devil's ivy' (Scindapsus aureus) is also recommended.

BELOW This lush grouping gets its drama from the bold leaves and strong contrast of colour and variegations of dieffenbachia, calathea and draceana.

DESIGNERS NOTE BOOK:

LIVING ROOMS

RIGHT The irregular, fluid lines of a single specimen plant, such as the dragon tree, can provide relief from the strong horizontal and vertical lines of modern decors.

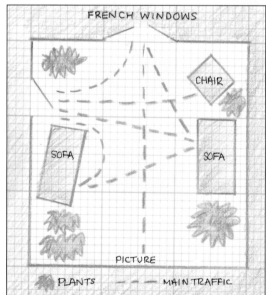

ABOVE Before you go out to buy large plants for an important room, draw up a simple floorplan of the room, with furniture, windows, paintings and traffic patterns indicated so that you can see what limitations and possibilities the room provides you with.

1 Caladium and Croton like warmth, bright light and humidity.

2 With good light the flowers on Hydrangea and Azalea last a couple of months.

3 The Dumb Cane needs heat and humidity; and Busy Lizzie should have its dead flowers removed every day.

4 Put a tender Prayer Plant on top of the mantelpiece where it can get reasonable light.

5 Grow Ferns in the light shade by the mantelpiece, but block off the shaft to stop draughts.

6 On a table out of direct light, you can put short-term flowering plants such as Begonias, Italian Bellflower and Cineraria.

7 A Weeping Fig is easy to grow, so long as it is kept warm. But it is much healthier if its leaves are often sprayed and cleaned.

ABOVE Real plant lovers will not mind fussing a bit with their plants and so can incorporate more demanding plants in their schemes. They will be rewarded for their efforts with plants of striking shapes, textures and colours. Care must be taken to choose locations where the plants' specific light and humidity requirements can be maintained.

1 A shade-loving plant here will be over-exposed to sun in summer. Plants here may get frozen in winter when the curtains are closed at night

2 A trailing plant dangling over a fireplace that is used may get scorched.

3 A plant that sits on top of a television set may get too warm — drying out the leaves and compost.

4 This plant may be in a draught, and may get knocked over or trodden on.

5 A plant here may not get enough light. It is far too cramped and the radiator will singe the leaves.

6 The radiator may overheat the trailing stems, possibly singeing them, and will dry out all the humidity. The draught from the door may brown the plant's leaves.

7 This plant may be scorched by the radiator, knocked by people coming in and out of the door and subjected to draughts.

ABOVE Points to keep in mind when placing your houseplants.

ABOVE Suggestions for making your fireplace the focal point of the room, when it is not being used.

2

IDEAS FOR DINING ROOMS AND BEDROOMS

LEFT A diverse grouping of smaller plants in varied containers is perfectly in harmony with the gentle, traditional atmosphere of this bedroom.

ABOVE All of these plants contrast beautifully with the highly polished furniture. On the table is the urn plant, in flower for many months. On the mantelpiece is a variegated vriesia, while the feather specimen is the Norfolk Island pine.

Plants add drama to a dining room, as a point of punctuation on a side table or on the floor, or as the dining table centrepiece. Foliage plants, either a group of them or one single bushy specimen, can make lovely substitutes for a cut flower centrepiece. A centrepiece of potted flowering plants gives you the fresh blooms and lovely colours of cut flowers but last longer. And some potted flowering plants, once the blooms have faded, can get a second life out in your garden, where they may flower again after a period of dormancy. (This is most true of flowering plants that have not been forced to bloom by being kept in hot greenhouses; such plants generally are all spent by the time their flowers bloom and are best relegated to the compost heap.)

It's usually best to remove a large centrepiece from the table during the meal to make room for the food and to allow diners to easily see one another across the table. But very small potted plants, as a grouping or several individual ones set thoughtfully around the table, can accent the place settings, bringing out colours and adding warmth and intimacy to the meal. This makes an interesting change from a vase of flowers on the table.

Sideboards and serving tables, usually filled with china and glassware, may have a spot free for a small plant. If a china cabinet has lighting fixtures inside above the shelves you may have a perfect place for a little plant that is happy without full sun.

LEFT This hanging container holds a young specimen of abutilon, with yellow flowers. This plant needs very light conditions if it is to flower well. Eventually it will grow too large and can then be used as a table or floor specimen.

BELOW An earth star coupled with a seashell that echoes its shape creates a small bit of drama that would be suitable for any quiet place.

29

The same dining table looks quite different for the evening meal. Its new yellow colour scheme is highlighted by the golden slipperwort that now takes centre stage.

ABOVE LEFT The simple addition of coloured napkins picks up the green in the mixed foliage plant centrepiece on this informal dining table, set for breakfast.

Then there may be window sills for plants or even glass shelves in front of a window. Don't forget the possibility of hanging plants. There is nothing more pleasant than coming down to breakfast to a room filled with plants basking in the sunlight.

Bedrooms are quieter rooms that rarely want or deserve big splashes of plants. But a few quiet ones here and there can add serenity where it's welcome. Little plants potted in small, ornamental pots are lovely at the bedside table, beside the lamp, the phone, the potpourri. For a charming effect look for unusual containers to use as pots: delicate porcelain teacups, antique silver boxes, pewter porringers, small wooden or cardboard boxes that you've covered in a fabric that matches your curtains. Varied groupings of such containers add individuality to your room.

Both dining rooms and bedrooms are usually moderately heated areas where the atmosphere is a little more humid than living rooms. They also tend to be more airy. The maximum temperature ranges from about 15.5 to 18°C (60 to 65°F), dropping to a minimum at night, of 10 to 13°C (50 to 55°F). Consequently, a wide range of plants can be grown in these rooms and you do not have to be quite so concerned about supplying extra humidity. Nevertheless, you can ensure that some plants live in a constant, moist atmosphere by filling the space between their pots and pot holders with dampened peat or other moisture-retaining medium, as described in chapter 1, or by mist-spraying the foliage.

Plants in bedrooms, like all plants, take carbon dioxide from the air and give back oxygen; there is no need to remove them from the room at night.

RIGHT Imagine yourself being greeted at breakfast by such a lovely window display. The two upper rows of plants here appear suspended in air but are really resting on glass shelves.

LEFT Tall potted plants fill these windows and create a beautiful, quiet place in which to dine. In winter the plants will be moved to a location away from the radiator because its heat will harm the plants, especially the thatch palm immediately in front of the heat. The large cissus (left) is a trailing plant that is supported by canes.

SPECIMEN PLANTS

Dining rooms, like living rooms, are often used for welcoming guests and are often larger spaces than other rooms in your house. For these reasons, they are particularly good places for a few large, bold specimen plants. Here are some to consider.

1 Abutilon striatum 'Thompsonii'. This is a shrubby plant whose big, maple-like leaves are heavily variegated with yellow. It is quite a tall grower, but it can be pruned back in early spring, when it grows into a much more bushy specimen. It can be placed outdoors during the summer. It needs plenty of light.

2 Aechmea fasciata ('urn plant'). This is not a particularly tall plant, but it could be placed on a pedestal to gain extra height. However, it is a very bold, striking subject. Its broad leaves are banded grey-green and it has a blue-and-pink flower head. The leaves form a "vase", which should be kept filled with fresh water. It needs plenty of light and high humidity.

3 Agave americana ('century plant'). This succulent plant grows a large rosette of sword-like leaves with spiny edges. Of this species the 'Marginata', with its yellow-edged leaves, is one of the most popular varieties. It needs good light and sun and prefers a dry atmosphere.

4 Araucaria excelsa ('Norfolk Island pine'). In its natural habitat this plant grows into a large tree, but it is a slow grower and is unlikely to exceed 2m (6ft) in height when grown in a pot. It resembles a Christmas tree and thrives in a moderately shady spot with a humid atmosphere.

5 Chamaerops humilis ('European fan palm'). This palm, which gets its nickname from its fan-like fronds, is easy to grow. It will not reach a great height and is therefore best suited to small rooms. It will grow well in a shady corner, but likes high humidity in warm conditions.

6 Dracaena draco ('dragon tree'). Eventually this tree (which does not grow very tall) forms a thick trunk, which supports its sword-shaped, bluish-grey leaves. It is very distinctive and is easy to look after, since it thrives in either bright light or moderate shade.

7 Monstera deliciosa ('Swiss cheese plant'). This popular houseplant (described in chapter 1) is very adaptable and suits most rooms. When conditions are warm, it needs a good supply of humidity.

8 Neoregelia carolinae 'Tricolor'. This is one of the bromeliads (like the urn plant) and owes its popularity to its colourful foliage. To give it extra height it should be placed on a pedestal. Its rosette of leaves forms a "vase", which must be kept filled with fresh water. The leaves are striped with green, pink and cream and the centre of the plant is bright pink. It needs very good light, and high humidity in warm conditions.

9 Strelitzia reginae ('bird of paradise flower'). This is an unusual plant for a room specimen and easy to maintain. It has huge leaves, similar to those of a banana, and a blue-and-orange flower head, shaped like a bird's head. The plant will not flower until it is at least five years old, but it is worth growing for its foliage alone. It needs good light and sunshine and can be left outdoors during the summer.

Yucca elephantipes. Tall, bare-stemmed houseplants like yucca are in vogue. Quite large specimens can be bought at garden centres and florists. It has a thick trunk, at the top of which is a cluster of upright, sword-shaped leaves. It needs no additional humidity, but must have plenty of good light.

RIGHT The bowl on the chest of drawers contains primulas, spider plants and ivies. On the floor stands a cabbage palm and on the window sill sits a white-sails plant, which flowers over a long period.

BELOW A delicate grouping of foliage plants, punctuated by a colourful African violet, kalanchoe and cyclamen, graces a bedroom window.

SEASONAL GROUPS

A group or two of mainly flowering pot plants, matching the seasons, provide an attractive and long-term feature in a dining room. They can also be arranged in planters (see the section, Groups in Large Planters in chapter 1). There are many combinations of flowering and foliage plants that go well together, but to get you started, here are a few that are highly recommended. All of them need good light.

In winter, the right combination of colourful plants can cheer up a room. An excellent winter plant, which can be kept from year to year, is the Indian azalea, correctly called *Rhododendron simsii*. It is an evergreen shrub which smothers itself with pink, red, mauve, purple or white flowers. Florists' cyclamen adds a special touch when grouped with the azalea. It has flowers in shades of red, pink or white and often the foliage is attractively marked

ABOVE Most bedrooms do not have room for large plants, but this one, with its French doors and large floor-to-ceiling windows, is perfect for big, splashy plants. The lace curtains are drawn during the brightest times of the day to filter out the sun that is too strong for many foliage plants.

with silver. A cyclamen, too, can be kept for several years. You will need some foliage plants to blend with these, such as the asparagus fern, *Asparagus densiflorus* 'Sprengeri' (described in chapter 1) and the 'spider plant' (*Chlorophytum comosum* 'Variegatum'), with its grassy, green-and-white striped leaves.

A good basis for a spring group are the primulas, such as *P. obconica,* with flowers in white and various shades of pink, red and mauve, and the fairy primrose, *P. malacoides,* which blooms in a similar range of colours. Both are discarded after flowering. For contrast, add a small plant of the silk oak (*Grevillea robusta*), with its mid-green and very ferny foliage, or the mother fern (*Asplenium bulbiferum*), which carries tiny plants on its fronds. (These can be used for propagation.) Some variegated ivies, such as the *Hedera helix* species, can be trailed over the edge of the planter.

For a summer group you might consider using a blue hydrangea as a centrepiece. The large blooms last a long time and you can treat it as a temporary houseplant and put it in the garden after flowering. Foliage plants which contrast well with the hy-

drangeas are the spider plant, the variegated, large-leaved ivy, *Hedera canariensis* 'Variegata' (for the edge of the planter) and *Fatsia japonica,* the Japanese aralia, with its large, evergreen, hand-shaped leaves in deep shiny green.

PLANT TREES

A well-branched cutting from a tree, supported in a pot, makes an ideal home for some houseplants, especially those which live on trees in the wild, like air plants. Several varieties of bromeliads can be grown in this way, too; they are particularly striking for their variegated leaves and, in some, their flowers. A plant tree makes a superb and unusual feature – even a conversation piece – for a dining room or another room where a single specimen plant will look good.

An ideal tree cutting should be well branched and can be of any height, depending on how prominent you want it to be. Remember to check that the branch is not rotting! You will need a clay pot to support the branch, preferably one of the fancy decorated pots. Place the branch in the centre of the pot and support it, temporarily, in an upright position. Then fill the pot almost to the top with mortar (a mixture of cement and sand). When the mortar has hardened, remove the supports. Position the plant tree where it will get plenty of light and stand the pot on a shallow drip tray. The surface of the mortar can be covered with a layer of peat or shredded bark to give a more pleasing appearance.

The method of fixing plants to the tree depends on the types you have chosen. Air plants (the small, atmospheric tillandsias), should be either carefully wedged at the base of branches or loosely tied into position, anywhere on the tree, with nylon thread. You can also buy a special glue for sticking the plants to the branches but make sure you use this type of glue only; any other may damage your plants.

Unlike air plants, epiphytic plants have roots and are bought in pots. To mount these on the tree, remove the pots and tease away most of the soil from around the roots. Then wrap the roots in live sphagnum moss and secure them to the tree with nylon thread, very thin copper or plastic-coated wire. The top of the plant may also need to be tied to the tree; if so, use nylon thread, making sure that it is as inconspicuous as possible. Always start off with small, young plants, which are easier to mount than large specimens. They will eventually make new roots which will attach themselves to the tree, enabling the plants to support themselves.

Since plants on a tree cannot be watered in the normal way, they must be supplied with sufficient moisture by a small hand sprayer of the kind used indoors. Spray the foliage of the plants, the moss, and the tree itself. Air plants will need spraying daily in warm conditions, weekly if the room is cool. Other plants need to be kept reasonably moist so spray as necessary. Air plants need only a light spraying each time, make sure not to saturate them. Use soft or lime-free water for air plants and preferably for epiphytic plants as well. Collect rainwater in a suitable container if your tapwater is hard or limy.

Liquid feeds can also be applied with the sprayer — about once every four weeks during the summer and at about a quarter of the recommended strength. Spray the leaves only with fertilizer. Spray-

ing can also cause drips and so it is best to stand the pot on a drip tray of suitable size or to lay down newspaper.

The air plants, or atmospheric tillandsias, are perhaps the ideal subjects for a plant tree. Some species are available from garden centres and florists, but for a wider selection go to a specialist nursery. Some of the better-known species are these: *Tillandsia argentea,* with thin, silver foliage;

ABOVE White porcelain figurines, a miniature picture frame, a tiny jug and small cups, mixed with white flowers and green foliage, have been lovingly arranged in this delicate bedroom grouping.

LEFT It is the range of pinks, offset by white and green, that makes this arrangement so successful. It will certainly brighten any dull corner or cheer up any sickroom. The flowers include cyclamen, geranium and cineraria. The tall foliage plant in the back is bird's nest fern.

T. baileyi and *T. butzii,* bulb-shaped, with twisted leaves; *T. caput-medusae,* also bulbous with twisted leaves; *T. ionantha,* with a rosette of green or silvery leaves; *T. juncea,* with rush-like leaves, and *T. usneoides* ('Spanish moss'), with a mass of grey-green, thread-like, pendulous stems.

Other plants suitable for a tree include the 'stag's horn fern', *Platycerium bifurcatum,* with antler-like fronds, and several bromeliads. The following bromeliads can be recommended: *Tillandsia cyanea,* popularly known as the 'pink quill', with a rosette of arching green leaves and striking blue-and-pink flower heads; *Vriesia fenestralis,* whose green-netted leaves form a water-holding vase; *Vriesia splendens,* or 'flaming sword', of similar habit, but with brown-banded leaves and a scarlet-and-yellow flower head; and *Guzmania lingulata,* whose glossy, green leaves have fine purple stripes and whose flower head is a spectacular orange and red.

LEFT Red carnation, poinsettia, kalanchoe and winter cherry bring Christmas cheer to a group of foliage plants.

ABOVE Both plants and people appreciate the natural light that pours through the skylight in this attic study. The large plants are dragon trees.

WALL TRELLISES

An indoor trellis panel, mounted on a wall, can be used to support plants in pot holders or climbing houseplants. It makes a dramatic and unusual feature for a dining room and often fits particularly well into an alcove where there is little room for anything else.

If the garden centres you visit don't have a trellis like you see here that is made especially for hanging pots indoors, you could look in stores that carry kitchenware or bathroom accessories. There you may find a plastic-coated wire grid unit made for hanging up towels, pots and pans, utensils, soap dishes or whatever. If the brackets sold for such units don't suit your pots, you can hang the planters from the grid with nylon thread or wire.

Such trellises are best hung on walls made of brick, stone, sealed wood or well-sealed plaster. Wallpaper will probably be all right so long as it is a plastic-coated paper suitable for use in kitchens and bathrooms. Because you'll be watering the plants hanging on the trelliswork and because plants emit water vapour naturally, you want to hang them against a surface that will not be damaged by a little moisture.

A plastic-coated, steel trellis, ideally in white, is the best type to use indoors. It usually comes with nylon brackets for attaching it to walls. It is held about 2.5cm (1in) away from the wall. You can obtain plastic-coated steel brackets to support pot holders. They simply hook over the horizontal bars of the trellis. If you cannot find them at garden centres, they are easy enough to make from heavy-duty, plastic-coated wire. Simply make a circle of wire to hold the pot holder, and bend the two ends of the wire to make hooks.

Many plants are suitable for displaying on a trellis, some of them epiphytic. Try the following: *Billbergia nutans*, or 'queen's tears', with deep-green, grassy foliage and green, pink and blue flowers; *Epiphyllum hybrids*, or 'orchid cacti', with sumptuous flowers in various colours; *Gynura aurantiaca*, the 'velvet plant', whose leaves are covered with purple hairs; *Hypocyrta glabra*, the 'clog plant', with orange flowers; *Impatiens*, or 'busy lizzie', with a long succession of flowers in shades of pink, red or orange; *Nephrolepsis exaltata*, the 'sword fern', with arching, light-green fronds; *Nidularium fulgens*, the 'blushing bromeliad', with a vase-like rosette of mottled leaves, red in the centre, and a red-and-blue flower head; *Platycerium bifurcatum*, the 'stag's horn fern'; *Rhipsalidopsis gaertneri*, the 'Easter cactus', with scarlet flowers; *Schlumbergera × buckleyi*, the ever-popular 'Christmas cactus, with deep pink or magenta blooms, and *Spathiphyllum wallisii*, or 'white sails', with white, sail-like flowers and dark-green foliage.

With such a collection of plants it is best to display them in a position where there is bright light. Humid-
ity should be provided by lightly spraying the plants with an indoor mist-sprayer. The display can be brilliantly highlighted at night if you install a spotlight.

Wall trellises can also be used to support climbing houseplants. Particularly suitable is the 'kangaroo vine' (*Cissus antarctica*), which grows about 2.4m (8ft) high. It has medium-sized, deep-green leaves. The 'grape ivy', *Cissus rhombifolia*, grows to a similar height and has lobed, dark-green foliage. Both can be grown in fairly dark corners or in bright light and both like moderate humidity so do not forget to spray the leaves.

Fatshedera lizei is a hybrid of *Fatsia japonica* and the ivy, *Hedera helix*. It grows about 1.8m (6ft) high and has hand-shaped shiny, deep-green leaves. It likes moderate humidity and can be grown in light shade and even quite dark corners.

BELOW Trailing plants cover a white brick wall. The plant pots are supported by individual brackets mounted in the brick. The brick is painted white, not just to match the colour scheme of the room, but also to reflect more light on to the plants.

DESIGNERS NOTE BOOK:

DINING ROOMS AND BEDROOMS

ABOVE Room dividers can make perfect places for houseplants. Glass shelving shows off the plants better and exposes them to more light than does wooden shelving. Choose plants that tolerate shade unless there is good artificial lighting built into the divider.

BELOW Window boxes need not only be used outside. Here terracotta window boxes sitting on an indoor window sill (lined with plastic film so that they don't leak) are planted with mother-in-law's tongue to form a sort of hedge. These planters would look just as striking sitting on the floor in front of a low window.

ABOVE A single tall specimen plant, like this yucca, can emphasize the height of elegant windows such as these.

ABOVE Potted flowers can echo the patterns and colours in wallpapers and soft furnishings.

ABOVE A large grouping of plants at the foot of a bed makes a bedroom a lush and romantic place.

1 A mantelpiece is ideal for an Ivy on the darker side, and a Scindapsus nearer the light.

2 In the direct light, grow a Spider Plant and a Castor Oil Plant.

3 A Jade Plant likes a lot of light, as does a Yucca.

4 In a slightly shady spot between two windows, a Mother-in-Law's Tongue will thrive.

5 An Aspidistra can sit safely in the darkest corner. Make sure it's not in danger of being scorched by the radiator in winter.

6 The door causes draughts, which are bad for plants. Also the constant flow of people in and out can damage fragile leaves, so keep your plants well away from here.

LEFT If you have houseplants primarily for their decorative qualities and want to treat them more as ornaments than living things, choose plants that are especially easy to care for. Those here fit that description because they need very little attention, so long as they are placed where their basic light and humidity needs can be met.

7 A Swiss Cheese Plant enjoys bright light but not direct sun. Give it a spot where is has plenty of room to spread.

3

·················

*S*PECIAL PLANTS
FOR BATHROOMS
AND KITCHENS

·················

LEFT The neutral colours of
this stylish bathroom
provide a dramatic
background for the
carefully placed plants and
matching green towels
and accessories.

RIGHT The bird's nest fern is a superb foliage plant and here contrasts well with an orange-flowered goldfish plant.

BELOW Typical bathroom plants. From left to right, aluminium plant, African violets in flower, and Begonia 'Tiger'.

Plants love bathrooms and kitchens more than any other rooms in the house. This is because these rooms are usually warm, and more importantly for plants, they both maintain a humid atmosphere. The maximum temperature usually ranges from 15.5 to 24°C (60 to 75°F), the minimum from 10 to 15.5°C (50 to 60°F). These warm, humid conditions are ideal for plants. Indeed, the bathroom and the kitchen are often the only places where enthusiasts can successfully grow the highly demanding African violets, or saintpaulias. These,

and many other exciting plants, are described below. You can also use any of the terrarium plants recommended in chapter 1.

There is little need to resort to elaborate displays or groups of plants in bathrooms and kitchens. You can show off plants as single specimens on shelves, on countertops or from hanging planters.

In the bathroom on a shelf in front of a mirror or mirror tiles is an ideal place since the mirror not only reflects highly beneficial light, it also gives the illusion that you have double the number of plants!

BELOW The bathtub surround is the perfect environment for many types of plants because it is often humid, and the occasional spray of water helps to clean the leaves.

BELOW No need to mount ceiling brackets for the trailing wandering jew and spider plant in this kitchen; just place them on the top of the cupboard. The potted plants around the sink need no saucers because they are resting on a stainless steel counter.

If you have a window in your bathroom, consider mounting hanging pots around it, or place glass shelves in front of the window and fill it with so many plants that they act as an effective window screen, making a shade or curtain unnecessary for privacy. Bathtub surrounds, if wide enough, are marvellous for ferns. They thrive in the humidity and benefit from periodic splashes from the bath and sprays from the shower. And ferns look lovely cascading over the tiles.

For the same reasons, ferns like to be around kitchen sinks (if there is room there) or hung above sinks in hanging pots. If you want to keep ferns in the kitchen, however, keep them away from the stove and be sure to have an exhaust fan near the stove because grease and cooking fumes are not friends to ferns, or other houseplants, for that matter.

Many cooks like to have some potted herbs growing on the window sill so that they are there, fresh and ready, when needed for a recipe. Herbs smell and taste wonderful but they don't always look wonderful, especially when they've been picked over. You can camouflage spindly ferns by mixing some bushy potted houseplants among them.

BELOW The wall unit displays suitable kitchen plants: Saintpaulias or African violets, the aluminium plant and Begonia 'Tiger'. The lower specimen is the goldfish plant. On the table, a young parlour palm enjoys the warmth and humidity.

LEFT An attractive bathroom setting for the maidenhair fern (left) and the bird's nest fern.

LEFT Special herb pots make these rather bland-looking chive, marjoram and thyme plants as pretty as they are useful in the kitchen. Strawberry pots in the background hold (left) miniature strawberry plants and (to its right) parsley.

ABOVE RIGHT The trailing fig on this kitchen window sill softens the hard corner edge and leads the eye down to a small potted azalea that adds a spot of soft colour to the otherwise neutral scheme of the room.

SPECIMEN PLANTS

Plants with wafer-thin leaves are ideal for window sills, provided they are protected from direct sunlight, which will scorch the tender foliage. Lights shine through the leaves, showing off their delicate patterns and enhancing their beauty. Here are descriptions of thin-leaved plants, including hypoestes, begonias and caladiums.

1 Adiantum raddianum ('maidenhair fern'). This is a very popular and dainty-looking fern, with wiry, black stems and small, fan-shaped, light-green leaflets. It needs plenty of bright light, but not direct sun, and it prefers a small pot.

2 Aeschynanthus ('lipstick vine'). All varieties have a habit of trailing and they look wonderful when they cascade over a shelf or window sill. And they all have flamboyant tubular flowers. The best-known variety is **A. lobbianus (A. radicans)**, which has red blooms. **A. marmoratus** has marbled foliage and yellowish-green flowers. **A. speciosus** has bunches of orange-yellow blooms. They need good light, but not direct sun. And they tolerate light shade.

Aglaonema ('Chinese evergreens'). These are lush, clump-forming foliage plants, which relish plenty of warmth and humidity. Their leaves are large, quite long and pointed at the tips. Some species have plain green foliage, while others are splashed with white, cream, silver or grey. The best-known species is **A. commutatum,** which has several strikingly variegated varieties. **A. modestum** with its plain green leaves, is another notable species. The Chinese evergreens are ideal for shady corners; avoid direct sunlight (page 68).

3 Asplenium nidus ('bird's nest fern'). This does not have a very fern-like appearance, but is nevertheless a handsome plant. Its long, broad, bright-green leaves are held more or less upright, in a shuttlecock-like formation. This is an ideal fern for shady corners. Never expose it to direct sunlight.

Begonia. Small foliage begonias are excellent for bathrooms and kitchens. Place them on window sills where the light can shine through the leaves, but avoid direct sun. Very popular are **B.** 'Cleopatra' and **B.** 'Tiger', whose leaves are attractively marbled with bronze. Also worth looking out for is **B.**

boweri, the 'eyelash begonia', whose leaves have eyelash-like hairs around the edges (page 66).

4 Caladium bicolor ('angel's wings' or 'mother-in-law plant'). This is one of the most beautiful, but also one of the most difficult, houseplants. Given high temperatures and equally high humidity, it will thrive; and if you cannot provide these conditions it would be wiser to spend your money on something easier. Alternatively, you could grow it as a short-term pot plant. Caladiums have large, paper-thin, multi-coloured leaves, featuring reds, pinks, whites and greens, depending on the type. They are perennial plants, grown from tubers, and you can buy them in the summer. The foliage dies down in autumn and the tuber should be kept warm and dry during the winter. Resume watering in spring and avoid exposure to direct sunlight.

Calathea makoyana ('peacock plant'). This is a low-growing, clump-forming perennial with beautifully marked foliage. Its long, rather broad leaves are boldly marked with deep and pale green and silver, and the undersides are purple. It is a slow grower and is best positioned in gentle shade, away from direct sunlight.

5 Columnea ('goldfish plant'). This is a trailing plant with exotic-looking, tubular flowers. Depending on which species you buy, the flowers are orange, red, pink or yellow. The well-known **C. gloriosa** and **C. banksii** have scarlet blooms. All of them need good light.

6 Cyperus alternifolius ('umbrella plant'). This is a sedge, a moisture-loving plant, with tall stems topped with an umbrella-like leaf arrangement. It can reach 1.2m (4ft) in height, but its dwarf form, **C.a.** 'Gracilis', does not exceed 45cm (18in). Stand the pot in a dish containing 2.5cm (1in) of water to keep the soil permanently moist. It needs good light, but not direct sunlight.

7 Dionaea muscipula ('Venus fly trap'). This is one of the carnivorous or insect-eating plants and will amuse kids and adults alike with its jaw-like traps, which quickly close together when an insect lands on them. It is a dwarf, moisture-loving plant and should be stood in a dish of water during spring and summer. It needs only barely moist soil in autumn and winter. It needs good light.

8 Hypoestes phyllostachya ('polka dot plant'). This is a bushy, small plant whose leaves are splashed and spotted with pink. It is shown off to its best when light from a window shines through them. Although it likes bright light, avoid direct sun. It is easily raised from seed; simply pinch out the tips of the young plants to ensure that it is bushy when fully grown. Never keep the soil wet, as this can lead to root rot.

Peperomia ('pepper elder'). These are popular, dwarf, clump-forming foliage plants, although they do produce thin spikes of white or cream flowers. They vary tremendously in leaf texture and colour. Popular species, found in virtually every garden centre of florist, are **P. argyreia,** whose largish leaves are striped with green and silver, **P. caperata,** whose deeply crinkled leaves are dark green, and **P. obtusifolia** 'Variegata', whose large, rather fleshy foliage is attractively variegated with green and cream. There is also a variety of the latter called 'Green Gold', whose pale green leaves are conspicuously edged with deep cream. The 'pepper elders' are ideally suited to gentle shade, and they must never be subjected to direct sunlight. One of the main causes of losses with peperomias is very wet soil, which leads to root rot; so it is best to apply water only when the soil is drying out. Be very sparing with water in winter. It is best grown in small pots, even if you have to allow plants to become potbound (page 69).

Pilea cadierei ('aluminium plant'). This is a dwarf, compact foliage plant whose oval leaves are heavily marked with silver or the colour of aluminium. It has a life span of only a few years and should be replaced regularly with young plants raised from cuttings in the spring. The dwarf, more compact, form is usually available from garden centres and florists. It is called 'Nana' and can be grown in a moderately shady corner, even though in winter it prefers better light. Like peperomias, the aluminium plant must never be overwatered; be very sparing with water in winter. Young plants should have their growing tips pinched out to encourage bushy growth (page 69).

Rhoeo spathacea ('moses-in-the-cradle'). This is a striking foliage plant which forms a rosette of rigid, lance-shaped leaves. Its upper sides are dark green and the undersides, vivid purple. It is best therefore, to place it where the undersides of the leaves are visible. Tiny white blooms, produced between the leaves, resemble a baby in a cradle. 'Moses-in-the-cradle' prefers a shady position and must certainly not be exposed to direct sun. The plant should be kept only barely moist during the winter. It prefers to be kept in a smallish pot.

Saintpaulia ('African violet'). These are highly popular houseplants, but their requirements – high temperatures and humidity – can make them difficult to grow. Try them in the bathroom or kitchen where the conditions may well be ideal. 'African violets' form attractive rosettes of velvety leaves and have either single or double flowers over a very long period, in shades of blue, purple, red, pink and white. Some forms have bicoloured flowers. It is important to note that some of the more modern varieties tolerate lower temperatures and are easier to grow. The 'Endurance' strain, for example, is happy in a temperature of 13°C (55°F). Although high humidity is needed, the foliage should never be sprayed with water. Instead, you should stand the pot in a dish of moist peat. Give it plenty of bright light, but not direct sun. It must be grown in a small pot so pot on only when a plant has obviously outgrown its container. Keep soil only moderately moist, and fairly dry in winter (page 71).

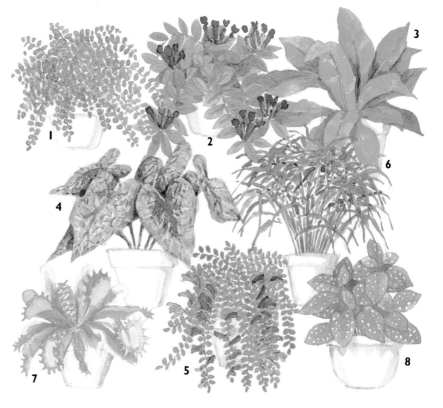

DESIGNERS NOTE BOOK:

BATHROOMS AND KITCHENS

LEFT Skylights can be wonderful places for hanging plants. This skylight faces north and brings soft light into the bathroom below, making it an ideal spot for ferns that enjoy both subdued light and the humidity of a bathroom.

RIGHT A mirrored wall can make a small room appear larger than it is – and it can show off houseplants. Here, a spotlight hidden behind the tall plant adds drama.

LEFT Palms and other plants that have strong vertical lines emphasize the grace and simple lines of a contemporary decor, while bushy, horizontal plants like ferns are more at home in an informal, homey room.

4

....

BRIGHTENING THE PLACE FOR VISITORS

....

LEFT Here, a variety of plants are brought inside to create a welcoming atmosphere, including a *monstera deliciosa* (on the left) and a rubber plant (on the right).

LEFT The cast-iron plant is one of the toughest houseplants available.

RIGHT The mother-in-law's tongue is very adaptable, thriving in sun or deep shade and low temperatures.

LEFT A colourful welcome for visitors is provided by a purple cineraria and a pink hydrangea. On the table is the Japanese aralia, a foliage plant; a yellow slipperwort, and white bellflower. Below is mother-in-law's tongue.

ABOVE The plants against the glass wall here have grown into a living screen that welcomes guests as they ascend from the entranceway on the ground floor.

First impressions are lasting impressions. A showy foliage plant at the front door, or a flowering potted plant brightening up the main hallway is a most welcome sign. Immediately it tells visitors that yours is a warm, well-cared for place, one in which they will feel comfortable and at home. Serenity is a feeling you yourself might like to have as you walk in your door after a long, trying day, and plants have an uncanny way of suggesting peacefulness. Around the holidays entranceway plant arrangements can silently wish guests a Merry Christmas, Happy Valentine's Day or Happy Easter (see the section Groups in Large Planters in chapter 1).

Unfortunately, the entranceway and front hall, along with landings and stairwells don't make for the best home for houseplants. There are draughts because of the many doors, and plants are subjected to gushes of cold air every time the front door is opened. What's more such places are rarely among the brightest parts of the house, simply because they are usually without windows. Thirdly, the temperature tends to fluctuate wildly between day and night. They are usually cool areas, often with a maximum temperature of 15.5°C (60°F), which drops at night to 10°C (50°F).

Tough, adaptable plants are called for, if they are to survive. Choosing these over fussier specimens will always be the safest way to go. But there are a few other things you can do to create more favourable conditions in such unfavourable places and perhaps

ABOVE This modern foyer is neither small nor dark, so it can use houseplants to their full advantage. The grape ivy trailing from an upstairs balcony softens the hard lines and surfaces of the space.

LEFT This dark hallway corner is brightened both by the white stairs and wall and by the lush plant arrangement.

have some luck with a greater range of plants.

Terrariums and other glass gardens might solve the problem of a draughty entranceway since the glass that surrounds the plants protects them. A hallway mirror will maximize any light that exists there; put a plant in front of it to take advantage of this. Short-term pot plants don't present problems; since they are thrown away after they have flowered, it hardly matters if the light is poor or the room is inclined to be chilly.

If your only choice is the most sturdy, common of plants, you can make them more interesting by planting them in striking planters. Brass and copper are bright and shiny, even in dull hallways. Pure white pots, against the glossy green of many sturdy plants, provide stunning contrast. And then there are other pots in dozens of colours that can be chosen to complement or contrast with colours of walls and flowers.

When hallways or landings need cheering up but are narrow with no room for planters or other furniture, hanging plants can come to the rescue. And stairwells can be really stunning with a large hanging plant cascading down it.

SEASONAL POT PLANTS

The plants listed here change colour during the different seasons of the year; and most of them are short-term, that is, they have used up all their energy and won't flower again. They should be discarded after flowering. Some, however, may be kept from year to year if you are prepared to give them a little extra attention. This will often mean helping them to go into dormancy for a while, just as they would naturally do if they were outdoors in their natural habitat. A dormancy period allows them rest and build up their strength for the next growing season.

Calceolaria ('slipperwort'). This is a colourful pot plant which is discarded after flowering. The inflated, pouch-like blooms, produced in spring and early summer, come in vibrant colours, such as reds and yellows, and the blooms of some types are spotted, in contrasting colours. If possible, provide bright light, but not direct sun. Keep soil steadily moist (page 66).

Chrysanthemum. The dwarf pot chrysanthemums are obtainable all the year round and are discarded after flowering. The blooms last for a long time, though, and come in various colours, such as shades of yellow, pink and red. Again, try to provide bright light if possible. The cooler the conditions, the longer the flower display will last (page 70).

Cineraria. This is a highly popular winter- and spring-flowering pot plant with a large head of daisy-like flowers in various shades of blue, purple, red and pink. Cinerarias are discarded after flowering. Try to provide bright light and keep the soil moist at all times (page 71).

Cyclamen. These are among the most popular autumn- and winter-flowering pot plants. The flowers come in shades of pink, red and white. Some types have very attractive, silver-marked foliage, others have scented flowers, and the miniatures are very charming, often highly scented. Try to ensure that the plants receive bright light. It is possible to keep cyclamen from year to year. They grow from tubers, which should be rested by withholding water between late spring and late summer. When watering, never wet the centre of the plant (page 66).

Gerbera ('barberton daisy'). Dwarf versions of these are now available and they are superb pot plants. They have large multi-coloured, daisy-like flowers during the summer and can be kept from year to year. They must be fairly dry during the winter. Provide good light if possible.

1 Hydrangea. The mop-headed hydrangeas are ideal for cool rooms and shady spots and prefer steadily moist soil. Plant in the garden after flowering (page 71).

Pelargonium domesticum ('regal pelargonium'). These popular and highly colourful pot plants bloom during the summer, the flowers growing many shades of red, pink and white. They can be kept from year to year, but it is better to raise new plants each year from cuttings, rooting them in late summer. Young plants must be kept in really bright light, but will grow in poorer light while in flower. Keep only slightly moist in winter (page 67).

Primula ('primrose'). Primroses are highly popular pot plants, flowering between late autumn and late spring, after which they are discarded. **P. obconia** and **P. malacoides** ('the fairy primrose') grow flowers in various shades of pink, red and mauve, and white. Dwarf, coloured primroses resemble the wild primrose, but flowers come in a wide range of colours. Provide good light if possible and keep the soil steadily moist (page 67).

2 Solanum capsicastrum ('winter cherry'). This is a popular plant for winter colour, with red or orange berries. Discard when the display dwindles. Keep the soil moist at all times.

Streptocarpus ('Cape primrose'). These are summer- and autumn-flowering perennials with funnel-shaped blooms in many colours. Allow them good light if possible. If you wish to keep the plants, place them in cool conditions throughout the winter and keep the soil dryish (page 67).

PERMANENT PLANTS

Plants listed here are tough houseplants that will survive for many years if given minimum attention and allowed to grow in a proper environment. Some have a trailing habit and their cascading foliage makes them quite nice for hanging planters or for placing on high shelves.

1 Aspidistra elatior ('cast-iron plant'). This is a clump-forming plant with long, broad, dark-green foliage. It tolerates deep shade, but grows better in more gentle shade.

Campanula isophylla ('bellflower', 'star-of-Bethlehem'). This is a trailing plant, ideal for hanging containers, with starry blue or white flowers in summer and autumn. It is best in bright light and you should prune the stems hard back when flowering is over. Keep only slightly moist in winter (page 68).

Chlorophytum comosum 'Variegatum' ('spider plant'). This produces tufts of arching, grassy foliage striped green and white. It is ideal for hanging containers. It will thrive in shade or bright light (page 68).

2 Clivia miniata ('kaffir lily'). This plant has large heads of orange, or orange-red, trumpet-shaped blooms in spring. Place the plant in the hall when it is in flower; at other times it needs good light and even some sunshine. Keep the soil only slightly moist during winter.

3 Cycas revoluta ('sago plant'). This unusual plant has a palm-like habit of growth and produces a rosette of rigid, shiny, deep-green fronds. It is a slow grower, achieving a height of up to 60cm (2ft). It needs bright light and should be watered sparingly.

4 Cyrtomium falcatum ('holly fern'). The fronds on this plant, which can be up to 60cm (2ft) long, are composed of large, slightly triangular, shiny, dark-green leaflets. The plant will tolerate shady corners, but prefers bright light. Only pot on this fern when it is pot bound, as it grows best in a smaller vessel. In cool weather, water sparingly.

5 Fatsia japonica ('Japanese aralia'). This ever-green shrub is hardy and can be grown outdoors. It has large, hand-shaped, glossy green leaves and tolerates either heavy shade or bright light.

6 Jasminum polyanthum ('jasmine'). This climber has highly scented, white blooms during spring. You should train the stems up canes or around a large wire hoop. Prune old shoots halfway back immediately after they have flowered. The plant needs good light and some sun, although it can be placed in shade while in flower.

Sansevieria trifasciata 'Laurentii' ('mother-in-law's tongue'). This is one of the most widely grown houseplants and is very adaptable. Its tall, spear-shaped leaves have yellow edges and it will grow in conditions ranging from quite deep shade to full sun. Water sparingly (page 70).

7 Saxifraga stolonifera ('mother of thousands', 'strawberry geranium'). This is an ideal plant to be put in a hanging container, with its rounded, silver-veined leaves with purple undersides and tiny plantlets carried on thin, pendulous stems 60cm (2ft) or more long. It is quite resilient and is suitable for very cool conditions. It will grow in either shade or bright light, but not in direct sun.

8 Scirpus cernuus ('miniature bulrush'). This comparatively new houseplant, with tufts of very thin, arching, vivid green leaves, is a moisture-lover so stand the pot in a dish containing 2.5cm (1in) of water.

9 Tolmiea menziesii ('pick-a-back plant'). A hardy foliage plant which can also be grown outdoors. The leaves carry young plants, making it a good choice for a hanging container. Ideally suited to moderate shade.

DESIGNERS NOTE BOOK:

BRIGHTENING THE PLACE UP FOR VISITORS

ABOVE Practically anything works as a plant stand so long as it doesn't overpower the plant and helps to create the mood you're striving for.

LEFT A dim, narrow hallway is made more interesting with this simple arrangement. The mirror makes the space seem bigger and reflects any available light on to the plant.

RIGHT Places that get little or no light can be temporary homes for plants. A pretty potted plant embellishes the foot of the stairs when guests are visiting but is returned to its regular home at a window a few days later.

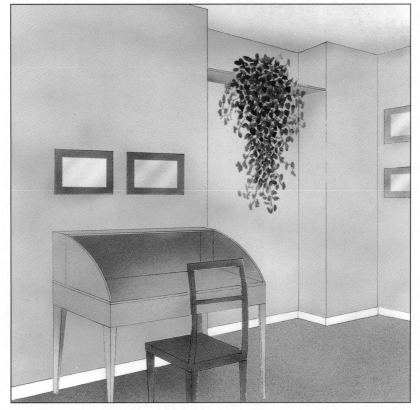

LEFT Trailing plants, like Plectranthus here, are often displayed in a hanging container, but they can also be shown off to full advantage when they are perched high on a shelf and left to cascade down.

5

················

HOW TO PLAN *YOUR COLOUR SCHEMES*

················

LEFT Only an all-white interior can handle the large collection of brightly coloured plants here. All but the foliage plants will eventually lose their blooms; some will then be discarded and others will be moved to the greenhouse until they flower again.

ABOVE There are plenty of plants with mauve flowers to match room decorations. Shown here is the hydrangea which is suitable for a cool room and flowers in spring and summer.

Probably more than anything else, colour sets the mood of a room. If you remember your early art lessons, you will recall that reds, pinks, oranges, yellows and certain shades of brown and beige are the warm colours. They make a room feel warm and friendly. (If the walls are painted or covered with one of these colours, the room may appear to the eye smaller than it actually is.) Blues, greens and some greys are the cool colours. They can contribute a feeling of lightness and serenity to a space. (And because cool colours give an illusion of receding, they can make the walls seem farther away than they actually are, so that the room appears larger.)

Of course the light in a room, and the size and shapes of objects in it, can play down or intensify

the feeling that colours give. Interior designers can explain all this better, and can help you anticipate the effects your selections will have. On your own, you will have to try some combinations and see for yourself how they work together with light, furniture and other objects, to transform a space.

Potted plants don't stay in bloom forever. Be prepared to move a plant whose flowers have faded, either out to the compost heap if the plant is completely spent, or to a sunny window, greenhouse or conservatory or the outdoor garden if it needs rejuvenation or a period of dormancy. For constant bloom, cheat a bit on nature and incorporate silk and/or dried flowers into a foliage arrangement.

Green, too, is a colour, and there are many shades

BELOW This arrangement points out just how colourful variegated plants can be. Two different varieties of prayer plants (left) sit next to pepperomia (right), with a Swiss cheese plant behind.

ABOVE Notice how the hint of mauve colour in the cyclamen flowers is repeated in the leaves of the rex begonia, in the tips of the seashells and in the mat of the framed print behind them. Such deliberate but subtle placement of colours brings harmony and rhythm to a simple grouping.

of green in houseplants to choose from and mix and match with other room colours. Place one green plant against another to bring out their differences. The foliage plants with variegated green leaves can be particularly attractive grouped together, to show off a variety of patterns and textures. Fittonia, maranta and peperomia are just a few of the many plants with striking variegated leaves.

Keep in mind as you choose plants to coordinate with your colour schemes that most all flowering plants and those foliage plants with variegated leaves require plenty of sunlight. If you are blessed with sunny windows, french doors, a skylight or a conservatory or sunroom, then you should have little trouble keeping such plants happy. If not, you may be better off sticking with green foliage plants and

using other things to bring out colours. As mentioned earlier, silk and dried flowers are colourful, and they prefer shady places, for will last longer without fading if kept out of the sun. Coloured pots can also add accents.

Forcing flowering bulbs indoors in winter will give you a spot of colour – and often scent as well – for a special place. Narcissus, crocus, hyacinth and tulips are popular for forcing indoors. Start hyacinth, tulips and narcissus in October and crocus in January. Plant a few bulbs in potting soil or compost. Keep the planted bulbs moist, on the cool side (although not cold) and out of the sun until shoots appear. Then move them to a sunny location. Once the flowers have faded throw the bulbs out, they will not flower again.

ABOVE Green and white dominate this room, but it is the splashes of bright pink in the potted flowers and the armchair that catch the eye.

RIGHT For a room with a green and white colour scheme, there are many suitable plants, both flowering and foliage kinds. This is the aluminium plant or pilea with silver and green foliage.

ABOVE Dozens of bright red geraniums, with bust sculptures hidden among them, create a strong garden theme in this dining room conservatory. Sometimes, as here, one strong colour repeated many times is more effective than a wide range of colours.

The quick-reference guide on the following pages covers the more colourful and distinctive flowering and foliage plants with a brief discussion about the conditions required by each.

Foliage colour depends upon the species and its method of culture. Apart from the full spectrum of greens, colours range from the various combinations of green with white, cream and silver of the variegated species to the blues and blue-greens, the yellow or gold tinged and the dramatic wine-reds, scarlets and bronzes.

Plants with variegated foliage will brighten a shady spot or illuminate an already bright position. Foliage or flower colours in a dining room or living room can be used to pick out the colours in china or table linen or to echo patterned upholstery.

RED

NAME	CHARACTERISTICS	TEMP. RANGE		HUMIDITY	LIGHT
1 *Aechmea* 'Foster's Favourite' ('urn plant')	Red-bronze foliage; forms a vase shape.	10–18°C	50–65°F	High	Place in bright position.
2 *Anthurium andreanum* ('painter's palette, 'flamingo flower')	Scarlet spathes or sail-like flowers.	12–34°C	55–75°F	High	Likes bright light.
3 *Anthurium scherzerianum* ('flamingto flower', 'pigtail plant')	Scarlet spathes or sail-like flowers.	13–24°C	55–75°F	High	Likes bright light.
4 *Begonia rex*	Large, multi-coloured leaves; red is usually dominant.	13–24°C	55–75°F	High	Best in slight shade.
5 *Calceolaria* ('slipperwort')	Large, pouched flowers; discard after flowering.	10–15.5°C	50–60°F	Moderate	Best in bright light.
6 *Celosia plumosa* ('plume flower')	Feathery plumes of flowers; discard after flowering.	10–15.5°C	50–60°F	Moderate	Best in bright light.
7 *Codiaeum* ('croton')	Large multi-coloured leaves; red often dominant.	13–24°C	55–75°F	High	Bright for best colour.
8 *Coleus blumei* ('flame nettle', painted nettle')	Multi-coloured leaves, lots of red; discard in autumn.	10–18°C	50–65°F	High	Bright for best colour.
9 *Cordyline terminalis* ('cabbage palm')	Long red and green leaves, palm-like.	13–24°C	55–75°F	High	Choose a bright spot.
10 *Cuphea ignea* ('cigar plant')	Long succession of tubular flowers.	10–18°C	50–65°F	Low	Bright, plus some sun.
11 *Cyclamen*	Flowers in autumn and winter, can be kept several years.	10–15.5°C	50–60°F	Moderate	Best in bright light.
12 *Euphorbia millii* ('crown of thorns')	Spiny plant with red flowers over a long period.	10–18°C	50–65°F	Dry air	Bright, including sun.
13 *Euphorbia pulcherrima* ('poinsettia')	Scarlet bracts in winter; discard after flowering.	13·24°C	55–75°F	Moderate	Bright position.

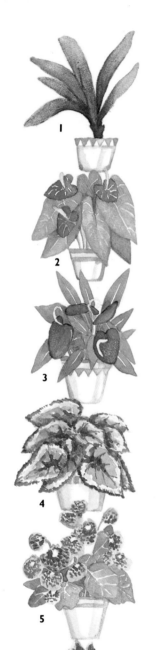

RED

NAME	CHARACTERISTICS	TEMP. RANGE		HUMIDITY	LIGHT
14 *Hibiscus rosa-sinensis*	Shrub with large, trumpet-shaped flowers.	13–24°C	55–75°F	Moderate	Bright position.
15 *Impatiens* ('busy lizzie')	Long succession of blooms; replace annually with young plants.	10–24°C	50–75°F	High	Bright or light shade.
16 *Iresine herbstii*	Wine-red foliage; replace regularly with young plants.	13–24°C	55–75°F	High	Bright, plus some sun.
17 *Kalanchoe blossfeldiana*	Red flowers in winter and spring.	10–18°C	50–65°F	Dry air	Bright, plus some sun.
18 *Pelargonium zonale* ('geranium')	Long succession of flowers; replace regularly with young plants.	10–15.5°C	50–60°F	Dry air	Bright, plus some sun.
19 *Philodendron* 'Burgundy'	Red-bronze leaves and stems.	13–24°C	55–75°F	High	Bright light or shade.
20 *Primula obconicia, P. malacoides* ('primroses')	Flowers in autumn to spring; discard after flowering.	10–18°C	50–65°F	Moderate	Bright position.
21 *Rhododendron simsii* ('Indian azalea')	Winter-flowering shrub; can be kept for many years.	10–18°C	50–65°F	Moderate	Bright position.
22 *Rochea coccinea*	Flowers during spring and summer.	10–15.5°C	50–60°F	Dry air	Bright, with some sun.
23 *Saintpaulia* ('African violet')	Violet-shaped flowers over a long period each year.	13–24°C	55–75°F	High	Bright for best flowering.
24 *Setcreasea purpurea* ('purple heart')	Trailer with vivid purple foliage.	13–24°C	55–75°F	Moderate	Needs a bright spot.
25 *Streptocarpus* ('Cape primrose')	Funnel-shaped flowers during summer and autumn.	10–15.5°C	50–60°F	Moderate	Bright for flowering.

24

25

23

21

14   15   16   17   18   19   20   22

WHITE AND GREEN

NAME	CHARACTERISTICS	TEMP. RANGE		HUMIDITY	LIGHT
1 *Abutilon ✗ hybridum* 'Savitzii'	Small shrub with white-and-green variegated leaves.	10–18°C	50–65°F	Low	Suitable for light shade or good light.
2 *Aglaeonema commutatum*	Foliage plant; some varieties with white-variegated leaves.	10–24°C	50–75°F	High	Ideal plants for shade.
3 *Callisia elegans*	Trailing plant with green-and-white striped leaves.	13–24°C	55–75°F	High	Needs a bright spot.
4 *Campanula isophylla* 'Alba' ('bellflower', 'star of Bethelem')	Trailing plant with starry, white flowers in summer and autumn.	10–15.5°C	50–60°F	Low to moderate	Choose a bright position.
5 *Chlorophytum comosum* 'Variegatum' ('spider plant')	Clumps of grassy green-and-white striped foliage.	10–18°C	50–65°F	High to moderate	Shade or bright light.
6 *Dieffenbachia maculata* ('dumb cane')	Large-leaved foliage plant; leaves marked cream and green.	13–24°C	55–75°F	High	Best in a bright spot.
7 *Dracaena deremensis* ('dragon lily')	Foliage plant with long leaves, striped green and white in some types.	13–24°C	55–75°F	High	Best in bright spot.
8 *Ficus radicans* 'Variegata' ('creeping fig')	Trailing plant grown for its white-edged leaves.	13–24°C	55–75°F	High	Bright light.
9 *Hedera helix* (variegated) and **10** *H. canariensis* 'Glorie de Marengo'	Trailing or climbing plants with green-and-white variegated foliage.	10–18°C	50–65°F	Moderate	Best variations in bright light
11 *Hoya bella* ('wax flower')	Pendulous plant with clusters of waxy, white flowers in summer.	10–18°C	50–64°F	Moderate	Provide a bright position.

WHITE AND GREEN

NAME	CHARACTERISTICS	TEMP. RANGE		HUMIDITY	LIGHT
12 *Oplismenus hirtellus* 'Variegatus'	Trailing plant with grass-like foliage striped with white, pink and green.	13–24°C	55–75°F	Moderate	Needs bright light.
13 *Peperomia caperata* 'Variegata' ('pepper elder')	Small foliage plant with crinkled leaves, broadly edged with white.	13–24°C	55–75°F	High	Bright light or shade.
14 *Pilea cadierei* ('aluminium plant')	Dwarf, bushy foliage plant; leaves heavily marked with silver.	10–24°C	50–75°F	High	Shade or bright light.
15 *Scindapsus aureus* 'Marble Queen' ('devil's ivy')	Climbing or trailing plant with white-variegated leaves.	13–24°C	55–75°F	High	Bright light.
16 *Spathiphyllum wallisii* ('white sails')	White, sail-like flowers and dark green foliage.	10–18°C	50–65°F	High	Best in bright light.
17 *Stephanotis floribunda* ('Madagascar jasmine')	Climber with highly fragrant, waxy, white blooms.	13–24°C	55–75°F	High	Needs maximum light for best flowering.
18 *Tradescantia fluminensis* 'Quicksilver' ('wandering Jew')	Trailing plant with leaves striped with green and silver-white.	13–24°C	55–75°F	High to low	Bright light for best colour and growth.
19 *Zantedeschia aethiopica* ('arum lily', 'calla lily')	White spathes or sail-like flowers in spring and early summer.	10–18°C	50–65°F	Moderate	Requires bright light.

YELLOW

NAME	CHARACTERISTICS	TEMP. RANGE		HUMIDITY	LIGHT
1 *Aphelandra squarrosa* 'Louisae' ('zebra plant')	Heads of yellow flowers; large cream-veined leaves.	13–24°C	55–75°F	High	Bright for flowering.
2 *Calathea crocata*	Deep yellow flowers; handsome green foliage.	13–24°C	55–75°F	High	Light shade.
3 *Calceolaria* ('slipperwort')	Large pouched flowers; discard after flowering.	10–15.5°C	50–60°F	Moderate	Best in bright light.
4 *Celosia plumosa* ('plume flower')	Feathery plumes of flowers; discard after flowering.	10–15.5°C	50–60°F	Moderate	Best in bright light.
5 *Chrysanthemum* (dwarf pot variety)	Dwarf bushy plant, flowering over a long period; discard after flowering.	10–15.5°C	50–60°F	Low	Bright for best flowering.
6 *Cadiaeum* ('croton')	Large, multi-coloured leaves; yellow often dominant.	13–24°C	55–75°F	High	Bright for best colour.
7 *Dracaena fragrans* 'Massangeana' ('dragon lily')	Long gold-and-green striped leaves.	13–24°C	55–75°F	High	Bright light.
8 *Heptapleurum arboricola* 'Variegata' ('parasol plant')	Hand-shaped, yellow-splashed leaves.	13–24°C	55–75°F	High	Place in bright position.
9 *Iresine herbstii* 'Aureoreticulata'	Yellow-veined foliage; replace regularly with young plants.	13–24°C	55–75°F	High	Bright, with some sun.
10 *Pachystachys lutea* ('lollipop plant')	Long-lasting yellow flower.	13–24°C	55–75°F	Moderate	Bright for best flowering.
11 *Peperomia obtusifolia* 'Green Gold' ('pepper elder')	Dwarf plant with pale-green leaves edged in deep cream.	13–24°C	55–75°F	High	Bright light or shade.
12 *Sansevieria trifasciata* 'Golden Hahnii' and *S.t.* 'Laurentii' ('mother-in-law's tongue')	Gold-variegated and yellow-edged leaves respectively.	10–15.5°C	50–60°F	Dry	Bright light, sun or shade.

YELLOW

NAME	CHARACTERISTICS	TEMP. RANGE		HUMIDITY	LIGHT
13 *Scindapsus aureus* 'Golden Queen' ('devil's ivy')	Climbing or trailing plant with gold-variegated foliage.	13–24°C	55–75°F	High	Bright light.
14 *Senecio macroglossus* 'Variegatus' ('wax vine')	Trailer or climber with cream-and-green variegated leaves.	10–15.5°C	50–60°F	Low	Bright position needed.
15 *Syngonium podophyllum* 'Green Gold' ('goose foot')	Trailer or climber with yellow variegated leaves.	13–24°C	55–75°F	High	Light shade.

BLUE

NAME	CHARACTERISTICS	TEMP. RANGE		HUMIDITY	LIGHT
16 *Brunfelsia calycina*	Bushy shrub with blue flowers in summer and autumn.	10–18°C	50–65°F	Moderate	Bright position needed.
17 *Campanula isophylla* ('bellflower', 'star-of-Bethelem')	Trailing plant with starry flowers in summer and autumn.	10–15.5°C	50–60°F	Low to moderate	Choose a bright position.
18 *Cineraria*	Daisy-like flowers in winter and spring; discard after flowering.	10–15.5°C	50–60°F	Moderate	Bright conditions
19 *Exacum offine* ('Arabian violet')	Dwarf bush plant with small flowers in summer; discard after flowering.	10–15.5°C	50–60°F	Moderate	Good light for best flowering.
20 *Hydrangea*	Large mop-like blooms in summer.	10–18°C	50–65°F	Moderate to high	Bright light or shade.
21 *Saintpaulia* ('African violet')	Violet-shaped flowers over a long period each year.	13–24°C	55–75°F	High	Bright for best flowering.
22 *Streptocarpus* ('Cape primrose')	Funnel-shaped flowers in summer and autumn.	10–15.5°C	50–60°F	Moderate	Bright for best flowering.

6

....

*C*ARING FOR YOUR HOUSEPLANTS

....

LEFT A vivid plant with shiny leaves, such as this painter's palette, is shown to best advantage with regular care and cleaning.

ABOVE Plants which need high humidity should be mist-sprayed daily if conditions are very warm.

LEFT When this bromeliad is actively growing the central reservoir should always be filled with water.

Few houseplants tolerate neglect or unsuitable conditions. Some will go on living when they are not properly cared for, but that is all they will do. They won't look particularly robust and they won't grow bigger or bushier. Houseplants grow and flower better if they are given regular care and an environment that meets their needs.

Earlier chapters of this book explained suitable growing conditions in each room for specific plants. This chapter is devoted to more detailed information on basic care of houseplants in general.

Plants in nurseries are kept in optimal conditions but can easily lose some of their good health before they are put on the shelves to be sold, or transported to secondary outlets like department stores, do-it-yourself stores, supermarkets and street vendors. So it always pays to give plants you're considering buying a quick inspection.

Common sense will tell you to choose plants that are clean and healthy-looking and to avoid any that have brown or yellow edges or tips, bruises or crushed leaves. Don't bother with any that are dirty or dusty or are sitting in dried out or excessively wet potting soil or compost. If you're selecting a flowering plant look for one that has some but not all its flowers in bloom. Those that are fully open will not last long and those that have only tightly closed buds and no flowers open yet may die before coming into full bloom. Pass by plants that have been sitting in hot sun, such as might be the case if the plant is sitting in a shop window or even worse, out on the pavement, unless you are sure that the plant thrives in full sun. The plant may not look sick now but might very well show stress after it's home with you for a while. Plants sold on the pavement not only have been often overexposed to the sun, they have also been exposed to gas fumes from passing cars and perhaps to draughts.

If you have a specific pot that you're buying a plant for, choose a plant that is already in a pot one size smaller than yours. This will give you a little extra room in your pot for pebbles or broken crockery for drainage and then an extra layer of potting compost or soil over that.

Unwrap any plant that is wrapped up so that you can check it over. But be sure that it is rewrapped or placed carefully in a bag or box before you take it out in the cold or wind.

And lastly, resist the temptation to choose a plant that you suspect is not suited to the environment in which you plan to keep it. It is far better to have healthy, good-looking common plants about than have to live with a sickly exotic one that will never look as good as it did when you first bought it. Before you go out to buy a plant you may find it helpful to browse through this book and jot down some plants that appeal to you and suit your home conditions. It's always easier to make a selection when you have some specific things in mind. If you forget to do this beforehand, you can always get help in making a decision from the plant care labels that should be tucked in the pot.

Once you get plants home, treat them as individuals. Check them over again for possible disease or pest problems. They may need a misting or some water right away. Large plants in small pots (often sold off cheaply) may have exhausted the nutrients in soil or compost and will probably benefit from repotting.

Here is a quick summary of important houseplant basic care. After this, on the next few pages, you will find more detailed care information. It will

BELOW The leaves of houseplants should not be allowed to become covered in dust or grime as this has an adverse effect on growth.

help you match plant or plants you have brought home to the lighting, heating, watering, food and care they require. A quick look at some basic rules:
— Don't give your plants too much water at a time and don't water too frequently; wait until the soil or compost is dry to the touch. More plants are killed by overwatering than underwatering. Most house-plants (unless care directions tell you otherwise) like to be kept on the dry side during the winter months, when they are in a dormant or semi-dormant state. This is especially true if the plants are kept in a cool room or a place a bit draughty; you'll find that they will tolerate such conditions better if they are watered only when their potting soil or compost is dry.
— Avoid intense sun, draughts, dry air and wide temperature swings.
— Fertilize your plants only during the growing season, which means during the spring and summer months. Feed every other week then. Only feed select plants (like some of the winter flowering ones) during autumn and winter.
— Repot about once a year, and more if needed. The best time to repot is in early spring when plants are beginning their active growth time.
— Keep plants generally clean. Remove damaged leaves often and give the plant a wash now and then. A shower in the tub or outside with a hose or watering can every once in a while will do. Fuzzy-leaved plants like African violets can be cleaned with a soft brush if you like.

Many houseplants need really bright light if they are to flourish. This means optimum natural light from the windows. Few houseplants, however, should be placed in direct sun, as this shines through the glass and will scorch the foliage. One or two plants do require direct sun, provided it is not too strong, and this is indicated where appropriate. Never grow plants which need optimum light in shady places or they will become weak and spindly, develop pale foliage and may never flower.

Many plants are suitable for shady positions, well away from windows, or even the quite deep shade that is found in the corners and alcoves. Plants which like shade will suffer if they are put in very bright light or sun, and the leaves will be bleached and scorched.

The brightest conditions are found on the window sills and within a metre of the windows. South-facing windows attract most sunshine and these areas can become very hot. Sun can be diffused with net curtains if necessary. Weak winter sun is rarely harmful to plants.

Plants which like really bright light, but not direct sunlight, are ideally suited to east-facing or west-facing windows, which receive very little sun. Light is also very good in the area of north-facing windows, which attract little direct sun.

Light coming from one direction only can make some plants grow or bend towards it, giving them a lopsided appearance. If this happens, turn the plants regularly so that each side receives a share of the light. Some plants, however, especially Christmas cacti, should not be turned when they are forming flower buds, as this causes the buds to drop off.

BELOW When repotting, handle the plant carefully to avoid damaging leaves or stems. This African violet is held below the leaves and gently tilted out of its old pot.

RIGHT One of the easiest ways to ensure humidity for plants that require it is to keep them in the bathroom or kitchen.

Most plants are happiest if the temperature remains steady, rather than fluctuating wildly. However, most of them can tolerate the difference in most rooms between daytime and night temperatures — rooms are generally warmer during the day — and each plant's temperature needs should be established before positioning it in a room. The day and night temperatures of a room are easily measured with a thermometer; do not risk guessing them.

Avoid subjecting plants to intense heat by exposing them to a radiator or a fire, as the leaves will become scorched or shrivel up. At the other extreme, avoid subjecting them to cold conditions. The space between windows and drawn curtains is a particularly cold area on a winter night. Plants should be moved further into the room before the curtains are drawn. Door and window-draughts can prove lethal to plants, causing leaf-drop or wilting. There are a few stalwarts (described in chapter 4) which tolerate draughts.

Humidity is the quantity of moisture held in the air. In a very warm room there is usually very little humidity, unless the room happens to be one, such as the bathroom and kitchen, in which water is used frequently. Cooler rooms tend to have a more moist atmosphere.

Many houseplants will flourish only in a humid atmosphere; if the air is too dry they may wilt or their leaves may shrivel and drop off or turn brown at the edges. Falling flower buds is another symptom of dry air. On the other hand, some house-plants, many of the succulents, grow best in dry air (as described in the tables in chapter 5).

To ensure high humidity you can grow plants in glass fish tanks or in the bathroom or kitchen. Alternatively, the pots can be plunged in peat or stood on a shallow dish or gravel tray containing peat, shingle or other moisture-retaining medium. These materials should be kept constantly moist to ensure that there is humid air around the plants. In addition, the leaves should be regularly mist-sprayed with water. This should be done daily if conditions are very warm. Plants which prefer moderate humidity will obtain sufficient moisture from moist peat, shingle or other moisture-retaining medium. In very warm weather they will also benefit from being mist-sprayed. Those which need only low humidity will be happy if mist-sprayed when conditions are very warm.

If you need to measure humidity, to ensure that your plants are adequately treated, buy a measuring instrument known as a hygrometer, or moisture meter.

Finally, you should remember never to spray plants when the sun is shining on the leaves. This can lead to scorching.

In this section, other important aspects of plant care — watering, feeding, potting, pruning, cleaning and general plant grooming — are considered.

Probably more plants are killed by being over-watered than under-watered. All too often owners give houseplants a daily splash of water, with the result that the soil or compost remains saturated,

HUMIDITY

GRAVEL

PEAT

GRAVEL

causing the roots to rot and eventually killing the plant.

Plants need more water in the spring and summer, when they are in full growth, than in the autumn and winter, when they are taking a rest. Indeed, some plants, particularly the desert cacti and succulents (not, however, the forest cacti, such as the Christmas cacti), should be kept completely dry over the winter.

Let us consider, first of all, how to water plants in the spring and summer. The best method of testing whether a plant needs water is to push a finger down into the soil, say about 12mm (½in). If the soil is dry at the top, but feels moist lower down, it is safe to water the plant. If, however, the top of the soil is moist or wet, then on no account apply more water.

Having determined that a plant needs watering, you will then need to assess how much to apply. This is very simple: the space between the surface of the soil and the rim of the pot should be completely filled with water. This will ensure that it seeps to the very bottom of the pot, so that the whole volume of soil is moistened.

When watering in autumn and winter, the soil should be kept only slightly moist. You can again determine with your finger whether watering is necessary. Insert your finger right down into the soil. If the top of the soil is dry and it feels on the dry side underneath then it is safe to apply water.

The correct amount is described above.

If you are not happy about relying on the finger test, consider buying one of the inexpensive soil-moisture meters. The meter has a metal probe which is pushed down into the soil and you can read the state of the soil on the dial of the meter, which indicates 'dry', 'moist' and 'wet'.

Some plants do not like hard or limy tap water and for them you should collect rainwater. Carnivorous and air plants are among the few groups of plants that object to hard water.

Watering is most easily done with one of the special indoor watering cans, most of which have a long, thin spout to enable you to reach out-of-the-way plants.

Unfortunately, many houseplants are not fed correctly. Some are overfed with far too much fertilizer, which can be harmful; and others are not fed at all, or only occasionally, which can also be harmful. We need to feed plants simply because they eventually use up all the foods or nutrients contained in the potting soil or compost. If they are not fed when this happens they will start to look starved and yellowish.

Plants which have recently been potted should not be given further food until they are well rooted into their new soil, which should take about six to eight weeks. Feeding should only be carried out when plants are in full growth, during spring and summer. Never apply fertilizers in the autumn or winter when plants are resting or growing very slowly, for they will not use the foods, which will then build up in the soil and harm the plants. During the spring and summer plants can be fed about every two weeks.

If you are inclined to forget to feed your houseplants, consider using fertilizer tablets. These are about the size of an aspirin, contain all the foods that houseplants require and are simply pushed into the soil as instructed by the manufacturer. The tablets slowly release the plant foods, over a period of several weeks as the plant is watered, and you do not have to use many throughout the growing seasons.

Alternatively, you can use a liquid houseplant fertilizer, following the maker's instructions. Some of them are seaweed products and all contain the minerals essential for healthy plant growth, nitrogen

LEFT Sponging foliage of a painter's palette to ensure shiny, healthy leaves.

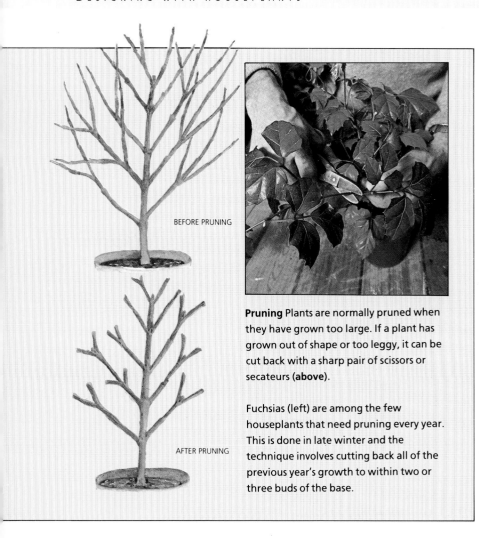

BEFORE PRUNING

AFTER PRUNING

Pruning Plants are normally pruned when they have grown too large. If a plant has grown out of shape or too leggy, it can be cut back with a sharp pair of scissors or secateurs (**above**).

Fuchsias (left) are among the few houseplants that need pruning every year. This is done in late winter and the technique involves cutting back all of the previous year's growth to within two or three buds of the base.

for foliage plants and potash for flowering species. They usually come as concentrated liquids which have to be diluted with water. One or two fertilizers suitable for houseplants, however, are available as soluble powders or granules, which have to be mixed thoroughly with water. On no account apply fertilizer if the soil is dry. First water the plant well and then give it a few hours to become fully replenished.

The majority of houseplants should be repotted regularly into larger pots – once a year if they are very vigorous plants. Repotting gives a plant more root-room and a fresh supply of potting soil or compost. Most plants, if allowed to become pot-bound (the pot tightly packed with roots), will grow poorly, or perhaps stop growing altogether.

There are a few exceptions, however. Some plants, such as African violets and 'pepper elders', have very small root systems and therefore do not need large pots. They should not be repotted until their pots are really full of roots and then they

should only be moved on to the next size of pot.

The ideal time to repot houseplants is in the spring when they resume growth. Then they will quickly root into the new soil.

In order to find out whether a plant needs repotting, remove the plant from its pot and inspect the root system. The easiest way to do this is to turn the pot upside down and tap the rim on the edge of a bench or table. The rootball should then slide out. If there is a dense mass of roots, with hardly any soil visible, then the plant can be moved on to a large pot. If, on the other hand, much of the soil has no roots permeating it, delay repotting perhaps until the following year.

A fairly vigorous houseplant can usually be moved to a pot two sizes larger. For example, a plant growing in a 10cm (4in) pot, can be moved to a 15cm (6in) pot. Slow growers and those with small root systems should be moved on to the next size. For example, if it is in a 10cm (4in) pot, it can be moved to a 12.5cm (5in) pot.

Pots of 15cm (6in) or less in diameter do not need drainage material in the bottom; larger pots can have a layer of broken, clay, flower pots ("crocks") placed in the bottom to assist drainage of surplus water. A layer about 2.5cm (1in) deep, topped with a thin layer of coarse peat, will suffice.

When you put a plant into a new pot set it on a layer of potting soil or compost and make sure that it is centrally positioned. Fill the space all around with more potting soil or compost, pushing down with your fingers. You must leave enough space between the soil surface and the rim of the pot for watering. The top of the rootball must also be covered with new potting soil or compost. The watering space varies from about 12mm (½in) to 2.5cm (1in), depending on the size of the pot. Water the plant well after potting in order to settle the soil around it.

Plastic pots are mainly used for houseplants, but you may find that large specimens grow better in the heavier clay pots; there is also less risk of their falling over.

There are two types of potting soil or compost to choose from: the traditional soil-based John Innes and the more modern, peat-based or soil-free potting soils or composts. The former have to be firmed moderately well when potting; the latter need very little firming and are lighter and cleaner to handle.

John Innes potting soil or compost is suitable for all plants, particularly for those which like a very well-drained growing medium, such as succulents and geraniums. There are three grades of John Innes potting soil or compost: No. 1 is used for potting young plants, such as rooted cuttings and seedlings: No. 2 contains 2½ times the amount of fertilizer and is used for general repotting: No. 3 contains 4 times the amount of fertilizer and is recommended for large plants.

Bear in mind that some houseplants, notably the Indian azalea, do not like lime or chalk in the soil. For these you should use an acid potting soil or compost, sold as 'ericaceous' potting soil or compost.

Few houseplants need pruning, although you can reduce the height of large specimen plants, such as rubber plants, if necessary. Dust the cuts with powdered charcoal. Climbers can also be pruned back, if they become too tall. This is best done in spring and encourages plants to branch out lower down.

There are a few houseplants which need to be pruned every year in late winter, notably hibiscus, fuchsias, pelargoniums and bougainvilleas. All of the previous year's shoots, which carried flowers, should be pruned to within two or three buds of their base.

Any shrubby houseplant may need careful trimming if it becomes too straggly. Trim just enough to maintain the plant's natural shape. If a variegated plant produces a shoot which carries plain green leaves, cut this out completely.

When carrying out any type of pruning always make sure you use a pair of sharp secateurs or pruning shears to avoid injuring the plant. Look for the growth buds on the stem and cut immediately above a bud or leaf.

Houseplant leaves should not be allowed to become covered in dust or grime, which harms their growth and makes the plants unattractive. You should regularly clean the leaves. Do this once a month with a sponge or soft cloth dipped in tepid water. Plants which have hairy or woolly leaves can be carefully dusted with a soft-bristled brush.

Houseplants with thick glossy leaves can be further enhanced by using a leaf-shine product. This makes them even more shiny, but you should take care to read the maker's instructions, as these products should not be used on all houseplants.

DIFFERENT METHODS OF CLEANING HOUSEPLANTS

There is no simpler way to keep your houseplants healthy and attractive than by keeping them well cleaned. However, you should be sure to choose the right technique for each plant, as leaves can easily be damaged by the wrong treatment. Hairy leaves such as those of the African violet should be gently brushed with a soft-bristled brush (a clean paintbrush would do), while smooth foliage responds best to sponging with water.

7

....

HOW TO ADD TO YOUR PLANT COLLECTION

....

LEFT The spider plant regularly sends out little 'spiders' or shoots, especially when potbound. These are very easy to pot up as new plants. For best results, root the shoots before cutting them from the mother plant. Do this by pinning them down with hairpins into moist compost or potting soil, or merely let them sit in cups of water until white tuberous roots appear.

Getting something for nothing is a wonderfully delightful idea – one that surely attracts a great many houseplant owners who have visions of new little plants popping up all over the place, ready to be potted up by themselves to keep or give away. It's comforting to know that an over-tall or leggy plant might again be as beautiful as when you first brought it home, thanks to a propagation method called air-layering. Or that your favourite plant, so robust and healthy, could become the mother of several more plants just like it, either by planting some of its seeds or by separating it into a few plants when it gets too big for its pot.

How nice to think you can fill your shelves with new plants without having to spend any more money – that you can raise plants for hostess gifts, Christmas presents, charity plant sales.

Getting something from nothing isn't just wishful thinking when it comes to some houseplants; many do indeed multiply all by themselves. Take the cholorphytum (spider plant), for example, which sets off little plantlets when it begins to get the least bit potbound. The Saxifraga stolonifera got one of its common names, mother of thousands (the other is strawberry geranium), from the fact that it, too, grows smaller plants readily. And Tolmeia menziessii (pick-a-back plant) grows plantlets from its central axis, giving the impression that these new plants are on the backs of the older plant leaves. All three plants can be kept as they are with their little offspring, and in such condition they make marvellous hanging plants. But you can very easily remove all or some of these plantlets and pot them up separately without affecting the mother plant in any way.

Lots of other plants can also be propagated and are fairly easy to do, even though there is a little work involved. Dividing pot-bound sansevieria (mother-in-law's tongue) into a few plants is easy enough, as is carefully digging out the offsets of bromeliads. Air layering a woody stemmed plant like the rubber plant or taking a leaf cutting from a begonia will involve a little coddling.

If propagating houseplants really appeals to you, then consider setting aside a place for a houseplant nursery. Choose a place that is out of the way of indoor traffic so there's no chance of plants being propagating getting bumped or knocked about. The space should have some sunlight, but it should be indirect or filtered with a sheer curtain or some such thing. Indoor grow lights do a fine job of providing controlled light when and where you want it. You will want to maintain good ventilation without draughts that can dry the air and stress the plants. Most propagating methods are more successful if the air is warm and more humid than normal. For this reason, a plastic tent or some sort of terrarium or glass garden can be helpful.

For all methods of propagation the use of a hormone growth stimulant or rooting powder will provide the new plant with a good start. Plants naturally produce these growth stimulants when they germinate and these substances, in low concentrations, produce the same effect on the rooting systems of new plants. Following manufacturer's instructions, they can be applied to stem, leaf or leaf bud cuttings and will ensure vigorous growth in the new young plants.

Many flowering and foliage plants can be raised from seeds, including temporary, flowering pot plants. Sow in the spring, using John Innes or soil-less seed planting medium. Small amounts of seed can be sown in 9–10cm (3½–4in) pots.

Sow as thinly as possible on a smooth, even, soil surface. Very fine, dust-like seeds can first be mixed with fine, dry, silver sand to make them easier to handle. These seeds must not be covered with soil, but should be lightly pressed into the surface with a flat piece of wood. Larger seeds can be covered with a thin layer of soil roughly twice their diameter, moisten the soil by standing the pots almost rim high in water.

RIGHT Dieffenbachia or dumb cane can be propagated from stem sections.

Seeds need warmth to help them germinate and this can be provided cheaply and easily with a small, electrically heated, window sill propagator. Alternatively, you can stand the pots on a warm window sill and cover them with clear plastic.

As soon as seedlings are large enough to handle easily, you should pot them individually into 7.5cm (3in) pots. Thereafter, repot as necessary.

Plants which grow a large number of side-shoots, such as impatiens, tradescantias, pelargoniums and beloperone, can be multiplied by stem-cutting during spring or summer. Use the tops of side-shoots, making the cuttings 5 to 10cm (2—4in) long. Then cut the base of each immediately below a leaf joint, removing the lower leaves. The base must then be dipped in hormone rooting-powder.

Insert the cuttings almost up to their lower leaves in a cutting medium; this is a mixture of either equal parts peat and coarse sand or equal parts peat and perlite. Firm the cutting medium around each one and water them in.

Cuttings also need warmth to help them root. Again, you can use a window sill propagator or you can enclose each pot in a clear plastic bag, supported with a few thin canes, and place it on a warm window sill.

When the tips of cuttings start to grow, this indicates that the rooting has begun; at this point, pot the cuttings in the same way as you would seedlings.

Some houseplants can be propagated from their leaves and the best time to do this is spring or summer. The same rooting procedures apply as for stem cuttings.

With some plants, saintpaulias and the peperomias, for example, you will need to use entire leaves, complete with stalks. The leaves should be inserted up to their bases in small pots of cutting medium. Eventually small plants will appear at soil level. If each leaf has several plantlets, try to separate them before putting them into small pots.

An entire leaf is also used for *Begonia rex* and *B. masoniana*. Remove the stalk, turn the leaf upside down and cut through the main veins in several places with a sharp knife or razor blade. Then lay the leaf, right side up, on the surface of the cutting medium and hold it down with a few small stones. Eventually small plants will appear where the veins were cut through.

With sansevierias and streptocarpus, a leaf should be cut into sections of about 5cm (2in) in length. Then dust the bases with hormone rooting-powder, making sure that you keep them the right way up, and plant them in the cutting medium. The top half of each cutting should be above soil level and must be watered well in. When the plantlets grow they should be bedded individually into small pots. (Plants of *Sansevieria trifasciata* 'Laurentii', raised from leaf cuttings, will not have yellow-edged leaves.)

This method is used for *Ficus elastica,* otherwise known as the 'rubber plant'. Cutting should be done during spring or summer. The rooting conditions recommended for stem cuttings apply.

BELOW The rubber plant can be propagated from leaf-bud cuttings or, more easily, by air layering.

A leaf should be removed, complete with a 2.5cm (1in) length of young stem. There should be a growth bud in the leaf axil – where the leaf joins the stem.

Treat the bottom of the stem with hormone rooting-powder and roll the leaf along its length; hold it in place with an elastic band. Then insert the stem into a pot of cutting soil, keeping the growth bud above the soil level. Next, hold the leaf in an upright position by means of a thin cane. Eventually the bud should start to grow and develop into a young plant.

This is an easy way of propagating plants such as the philodendrons, dieffenbachias, dracaenas, cordylines, aglaoemas, scindapsus and monsteras. They are all plants with thick, fleshy stems. The best time is spring or summer. The same conditions apply as for cuttings.

Choose a young stem and remove it completely. Cut off all the leaves, then cut the stem into 5cm (2in) long sections, making sure that each contains a leaf joint, or a node, which will have a growth bud. The bottoms of the cuttings have to be treated with hormone rooting-powder. You should plant them vertically, to about half their length, in pots of cutting medium. The buds will grow first, fol-

lowed a few weeks later by the roots. When this happens the cuttings can be put individually into small pots.

This is a very easy method of multiplying some houseplants, as it simply involves splitting them into a number of smaller pieces, complete with roots and top growth. You can do this with many clump-forming houseplants such as chlorophytum, ferns, sansevieria, maranta and aglaonema; but take care not to divide them until they are quite large. The best time to carry out division is in the spring, just as the plants are about to resume growth after their winter rest. Often it can be carried out during repotting, which is a convenient time.

Most plants can be pulled apart, after first teasing away some of the old soil. If this proves difficult, cut through the rootball with a sharp knife. The centre of a plant is usually discarded during division as it is old and feeble. Save the younger, outer parts for potting into suitable sized pots.

This is another type of division, used for subjects which produce young plants at their bases, as happens with bromeliads (aechmea, vriesia, guzmania, etc.). Many cacti and other succulents also produce young plants.

You must wait until the offsets are reasonably large before removing them. With bromeliads they should be about 15cm (6in) high. Offsets generally have roots, which should be removed with as much of the root system still intact as possible. Carefully tease away the soil to expose the roots before pulling away or cutting off the young plant.

ABOVE Crowded African violet plants can easily be divided so that each part can be planted in its own pot. Begin by removing the plant from its pot and gently easing sections apart.

Offsets should be potted individually into suitably sized pots and then kept in warm conditions for a few weeks to encourage them to root quickly in the new soil. Once they are established the young plants can be placed in appropriate room conditions.

Some houseplants produce young plants on their leaves or on the ends of long stems. These plantlets can be used for propagation.

The most common examples of houseplants which produce plantlets are chlorophytum, *Tolmiea menziessii* and *Saxifraga stolonifera*. You should encourage the plantlets to root into small pots of potting soil placed alongside the mother plant before removing them. Simply pin them down to the surface of the soil with a piece of wire bent into the shape of a hairpin. It will only be a matter of weeks before the young plants have rooted into the soil, when they can be cut away from their parents.

There is also a fern which produces plantlets on its leaves. This is called the 'mother fern', or *Asplenium bulbiferum*. To encourage its plantlets to root you should remove an entire leaf, or frond, in which they are contained and place it on the surface of the potting soil or compost. Hold it in close contact with the soil by inserting some wire pins (as described above). Keep the leaf in a warm and humid place, which can be provided by an electrically heated window sill propagator, and within a few weeks the plantlets will have rooted into the soil. They can be separated and put individually into small pots.

This is a fascinating and easy method of propagating certain houseplants, especially those kinds which become too tall for a room, such as *Ficus elastica* and other ficus species, codiaeums, monsteras, dracaenas and philodendrons. The method is reserved for woody or shrubby plants.

What we are aiming to do is to encourage the top part of the stem to produce roots before removing it. The best time to carry out air layering is in the spring or summer, when the plant is growing, and it needs to be done in warm conditions to ensure that the stem quickly forms roots.

Rooting should be encouraged approximately 30cm (12in) below the tip of the stem. You will have to wound this part of the stem in some way to induce rooting. First, if necessary, remove a few leaves from the area. Then cut a 5cm (2in) long tongue in the stem, using a sharp knife. Make the cut in an upward direction and make sure that the knife penetrates halfway through the stem. The cut surfaces of this tongue should then be dusted with hormone rooting-powder, which further helps to encourage roots to grow. The tongue should be kept open by packing it with sphagnum moss, which must be moist.

If you find that cutting a tongue is too difficult, a simpler method of wounding the stem is to remove completely a ring of bark, no more than 12mm (½in) wide. Again, dust the wound with hormone rooting-powder. The part of the stem which has been wounded should then be wrapped with reasonably moist sphagnum moss. The moss has to be held in place by wrapping it with a square of clear plastic sheeting. Each end of this bandage should be secured and sealed with adhesive tape. Run a length of tape along the overlap, too.

The length of time that the stem takes to produce roots depends on the temperature maintained and the kind of plant you use. However, you will know when an adequate root system has formed as white roots will be seen through the plastic.

At this stage remove the plastic bandage. It is recommended that the moss be left in place; removing it may damage the young roots, which can be somewhat brittle.

Remove the top of the stem just below the rooted area and pot it in a suitably sized pot. It is best to keep the newly potted plant in a warm and humid place until it has established itself in its pot. Only then can it be moved to normal conditions.

Naturally, you will be left with a beheaded plant, although there is no reason why you should not keep it. It is recommended that you prune the plant hard back; you can safely remove half to two-thirds of the remaining stem. Eventually the plant will branch out and become quite bushy.

LEFT Pepperomias are raised from leaf cuttings.

8

....

HOW TO OVERCOME PROBLEMS

....

LEFT Regular inspection of your plants is vital to catch any pests or diseases in the early stages.

Comparatively few pests and diseases attack houseplants, unlike their less fortunate relatives in the garden, and it is probably safe to say that more problems are caused by cultural faults such as draughts, dry air and over-watering or under-watering than by anything else.

As in so many other things, its much easier to prevent a problem than to cure one. In addition to maintaining the growing conditions you know your plants like, pull off dead and sickly leaves when you see them, prune off weak stems if you can and repot when necessary. If, despite these measures, a plant gets sick, isolate it immediately from its neighbours. Insects and certain diseases can spread from one plant to another.

If you've given your houseplants a breath of fresh air by having them outdoors for a while, it's especially important to inspect them carefully before you bring them back indoors. They could have become home to garden pests or picked up a virus which could spread to other innocent houseplants. If you take your houseplants very seriously you might want to get yourself a magnifying glass and give your plants a closer look.

Thanks to chemical science, many problems can be dealt with, and on nearby pages you'll find suggestions for treatment, usually with aerosol houseplant pest-killers. Other pesticides can be used, too, but if they are not designed specifically for houseplants it is best to spray the plants in a shed or garage and take them back indoors once the foliage has dried. (It is also a good idea to use household sprays outdoors, to avoid overspraying on to healthy plants, food, pets and other living things.)

When spraying a plant with a pesticide, make sure that the undersides of the leaves and the shoot tips are well covered in spray, because pests often congregate in these areas. Be certain, also, that the plants are not exposed to the sun during the spraying. All pesticides are toxic, so handle them with care and always follow the manufacturer's instructions exactly.

If you're uncomfortable using toxic substances around the house, then discard the sick plant instead and buy another. A lost plant may be a small sacrifice if there is a danger of keeping a harmful substance around children, pets or even yourself.

Aphids

Mealy bug (closeup)

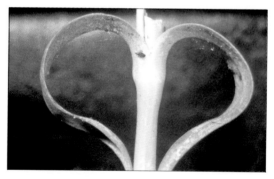
Red spider mite

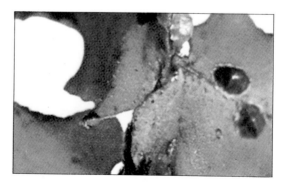
Scale insects

PEST

	CHARACTERISTICS/SYMPTOMS	TREATMENT/PREVENTION
APHIDS (GREENFLY)	Small green bugs which congregate on tips of shoots and young foliage. They suck sap, causing distorted growth	Spray with insecticide containing dimethoate or permethrin.
MEALY BUG	Larger bugs than aphids, but with a white, mealy coating, causing the same damage as aphids. They attack cacti, succulents and woody plants.	Spray with insecticide containing malathion or permethrin; or paint with methylated spirits.
RED SPIDER MITE	Virtually microscopic red spiders, which suck sap, resulting in very fine, pale mottling on the leaves of many houseplants.	Spray with insecticide containing dimethoate or permethrin; maintain a humid atmosphere around plants.
SCALE INSECTS	Insects that look like brown or grey scales; they suck plant sap without moving. They are found on the stems of many plants, especially woody kinds.	See mealy bug.
VINE WEEVIL	Larvae (small white grubs with brown heads) which live in the soil, feeding off the roots of various plants and the tubers of cyclamen. Plants eventually start to wilt.	Soil should be heavily watered with the insecticide, gamma-HCH.
WHITEFLY	Small white flies found on the undersides of the leaves of many plants, where they suck the sap. They produce an unsightly, sticky liquid.	Spray with insecticide containing permethrin.

Vine weevil

Whitefly

RIGHT Mealy bug

DISEASE

	CHARACTERISTICS/SYMPTOMS	TREATMENT/PREVENTION
BOTRYTIS	Grey mould found on the flowers, stems or leaves of many plants. The affected parts rot.	Affected parts of plant should, if possible, be removed. Spray with fungicide containing benomyl.
DAMPING-OFF	Disease which affects seedlings, causing them to collapse and die.	As a preventative, water new sown seeds, and seedlings after potting, with Cheshunt Compound. Always use clean containers and fresh potting soil or compost.
LEAF-SPOT	Fungal disease appearing as brown spots on the foliage of plants such as dieffenbachias, dracaenas and citrus. The spots can spread and kill the leaf.	Cut off badly affected leaves and spray with fungicide containing benomyl.
POWDERY MILDEW	Leaves and tips of shoots of numerous plants covered in white powdery patches.	Spray with fungicide containing benomyl.
ROOT-ROT	Very wet soil encourages a fungal disease which causes roots to rot. Early symptoms are wilting of the plant and yellowing foliage. The plant eventually dies. Susceptible plants include begonias, saintpaulias, cacti, succulents and palms.	Take care with watering. Examine roots by removing all soil. If only a few are rotting, remove them and repot the plant into fresh soil.
VIRUS	Diseases which cause leaves to become streaked, mottled or marbled with yellow, and often severely distorted. They can also cause general stunting of the plant.	Badly affected plants should be discarded, as there is no cure for viruses.

Botrytis   Leaf-spot   Root-rot

Damping-off   Powdery-mildew   Virus

CULTURAL FAULTS

	CHARACTERISTICS/SYMPTOMS	TREATMENT/PREVENTION
BROWN LEAF EDGES	A very common problem, usually caused by dry air. Draughts, and conditions which are too cold, can also cause brown leaf edges.	Increase humidity; mist-spraying the leaves will also help. Avoid cold draughts; place plant in warmer conditions.
BROWN SPOTS OR PATCHES ON LEAVES	Often these are scorch marks caused by the sun shining on the leaves. Scorching is more severe if the leaves are holding droplets of water.	Bear in mind that most houseplants should not be subjected to direct sun. Never spray plants if sun is shining on the leaves.
CHLOROSIS	Symptoms are yellow foliage and often stunted growth. Chlorosis affects lime-hating plants such as the Indian azalea if they are grown in potting soil or compost containing lime or chalk.	Use acid or lime-free potting soil or compost when potting. Use rainwater for watering. To cure an affected plant, water the soil with a solution of sequestered iron.
FLOWER-BUD DROP	This can be caused by unsuitable growing conditions; dry soil or air, poor light, or too high a temperature. Some plants such as the Christmas cactus also drop their buds if moved.	Ensure the growing conditions are correct for the plant. Pay attention to watering (don't let the soil dry out); decide where you want to display the plant before it starts to produce flower buds and then leave undisturbed.
LEAF CURL AND DROP	See wilting foliage.	See wilting foliage.
WILTING FOLIAGE	Many factors can cause the foliage to wilt: keeping the soil too wet or too dry; cold draughts; conditions generally too cold for the plant; wildly fluctuating temperatures; fumes from gas fires or paraffin heaters; and dry air.	Identify the cause and then rectify it.

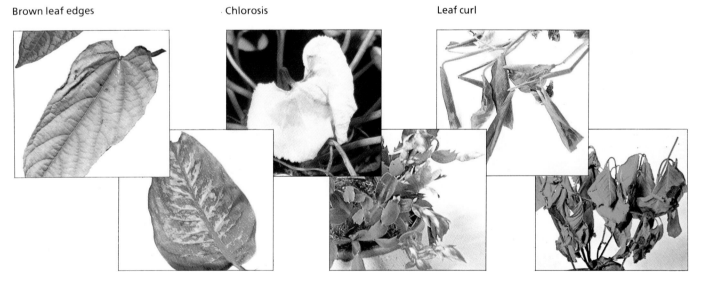

Brown leaf edges

Chlorosis

Leaf curl

Brown spots

Flower-bud drop

Wilting foliage

INDEX OF PLANT NAMES